amy butler's little stitches for little ones

by amy butler

photographs by colin mcguire

amy butler's
little stitches for little ones

20 keepsake sewing projects for baby and mom

CHRONICLE BOOKS

SAN FRANCISCO

Library of Congress Cataloging-in-Publication Data.
Butler, Amy.
  Little Stitches for Little Ones / by Amy Butler ;
  photographs by Colin McGuire.
     p. cm.
Includes index.
ISBN: 978-0-8118-6128-1
1. Infants' clothing. 2. Sewing. 3. Infants' supplies. I. Title.
TT637.B976 2008
646.4'06--dc22
2007038148

Manufactured in China.

Technical Writing by **Dianne Barcus** and **Kim Ventura**
Illustrations by **Jacob Redinger**
Designed by **Warmbo Design**
Styling by **Natalie Marotta**
Text and Projects by **Amy Butler**
Art Direction by **Amy Butler**

10 9 8 7 6 5 4 3 2 1

Chronicle Books LLC
680 Second Street
San Francisco, California 94107

www.chroniclebooks.com

acknowledgments

This book is dedicated to the sewing community at large. Without your enthusiasm and spirit, the fine craft of sewing would not be as vibrant.

Thanks to everyone who contributed to the making of this book. This creative adventure would not be possible without you.

A special thanks to Dianne Barcus, Kim Ventura, and Jake Redinger for your energy, creativity, and support in writing the instructions and illustrating the projects. I'm blessed to be able to work alongside you, and I am constantly inspired by your talents and abilities. My husband David for being so good to me always and for helping write this book. Diane Capaci for keeping the studio humming. Colin McGuire for his beautiful, warm photography and Anita for her positive support. Natalie Marotta for her incredible styling and vision. Anna Aschenbeck for her help with grading our pattern pieces. Sarah Amrhein and Joyce Robertson from Westminster Fibers for being so good to us and sending loads of fabric our way. Rolando Berdion from Pellon for keeping us stocked in printable fabric and interfacings. Janome Corporation for providing us with incredible sewing machines. Coats & Clark for providing notions and thread. Catherine Hurlbut from Fairfield for keeping us stocked in batting, Nu-Foam, pillow forms, and Nature-fil. Caroline and Marc for their constant vision. Sara Lorimer and Laurel Leigh for editing our instructions. Ayako Akazawa for her guidance and great attitude, Kate Prouty for her energy, support and patience. And Jodi Warshaw for her leadership, enthusiasm, and encouragement . . . working with you is a joy.

contents

(DIFFICULTY LEVEL: 1 = EASIEST; 5 = HARDEST)

introduction

Everyone loves to see a baby's eyes light up at the sight of familiar faces and objects. The idea for this book came from my love of making special treasures for the little ones in my world. I believe the most important possessions are the ones that connect us to the people we love. Creating what I call "modern heirlooms"—homemade items that are absolutely chic and up-to-date and that can be lovingly handed down through the generations—is the impetus for each of the sewing projects in this book.

While trends are always changing, the art of sewing remains timeless. When you make it yourself, a useful article is infused with your passion, style, and love—and you're no longer restricted to buying cookie-cutter, off-the-rack gifts! A one-of-a-kind toy, sewn from a favorite printed cotton, holds value and meaning for its owner that will only increase with time and use. Little stains and wear marks that will appear over generations of use will become part of a story you started.

The projects in *Little Stitches for Little Ones* are designed for babies 0–12 months. There is something for every little one, including a snuggly bedtime wrap blanket, PJs, cute booties and hats, a diaper bag and pad, imaginative soft toys, and even a soft fabric photo album.

There is something here for every sewer, too. *No matter what your skill level,* you'll find projects just right for you. Within each chapter, projects are organized by level of difficulty: #1 = easiest and #5 = hardest. And, *all* of the projects are achievable—even if you're just learning to sew!

I encourage you, especially if you're new to sewing, to begin by reading Getting Started (page 9). In this chapter, you'll find great tips on materials, tools, and fabrics, as well as measurement guidelines that will prove valuable. Refer to Glossary and Techniques (page 169) for handy sewing definitions and illustrated how-tos.

Little Stitches for Little Ones is perfect for modern women who wish to make unique items rich with meaning and emotion—cherished treasures that will retain their beauty through generations of cuddling, sleeping, playing, and yes, gnawing. Let your personality shine through each treasure you create, and always keep in mind my mantra:

Utility can be beautiful.
Comfy can be stylish.
Handmade is best!

Enjoy!
—Amy

chapter: 1.o getting started

We all know once babies take those first few hesitant steps, in no time at all they're walking with confidence. Similarly, learning to sew starts with baby steps.

This chapter will help you start off on the right foot (so you can finish that beloved baby treasure before the intended recipient is running from room to room or too big to wear it!). Here you'll find sewing basics, from choosing fabrics to taking measurements to selecting the best tools and materials. With a little patience and practice—and a lot of fun along the way—you'll be sewing with confidence.

FABRICS

Use your best judgment when it comes to baby's comfort (which should always come first). Durability, safety, and what I call "extreme soft factor" of fabrics are important. Pick fabrics you feel the baby (and if it's a gift, the parents) will love.

Use new fabrics whenever possible. You'll want these beauties to be much-loved hand-me-downs that last for generations. Quilting shops and fabric stores offer a vast sea of options. See Resources (page 175) for suggestions for where to start looking. You may want to purchase bedsheets and covers or tablecloths and repurpose them. I love to search for and combine vintage prints with modern designs.

I recommend predominantly mid-weight fabrics and quilting/fashion-weight cottons for the garments, toys, and decor projects in this book. Soft flannels and fleece are ideal for the cozy comforters and blankets. Certainly you'll want to stay with natural fibers (cottons, organic cottons, flannel cottons) and soft fleeces for baby's comfort. Avoid synthetics that don't breathe or heavy wools that might prove irritable to baby's tender skin. Choose materials that are easy to clean and easy to dry.

Be sure to wash and press all fabrics before you start cutting and sewing. This will ensure correct measurements and cuts. Most cottons and linens can be machine washed in cold water on the gentle cycle.

Here is a simple size chart to help you quickly select the proper size to make each project. Remember that babies grow quickly; depending on your sewing speed and the time you have to devote to the project, you may want to factor in baby's growth rate. Use a measuring tape to measure baby's dimensions; then follow the size chart.

Size Chart:

Size (in months)	0–3	3–6	6–9	9–12
Head	14"	16"	18"	20"
Chest	16"	17"	18"	19"
Belly	19"	20"	21"	22"
Length	21 ½"	23"	24 ½"	26"
Foot length	4 ¼"	4 ½"	4 ¾"	5"

Size (in months)	0–3	3–6	6–9	9–12
Shorts				
—Outseam	8 ¾"	9"	9 ¼"	9 ½"
—Inseam	3 ½"	3 ½"	3 ½"	3 ½"
Pants				
—Outseam	10 ¾"	11 ½"	12 ⅜"	13 ⅛"
—Inseam	5 ¾"	6 ¼"	6 ¾"	7 ¼ "

How to Measure Baby:

Head: Measure around the largest area, above the eyebrows and ears and continuing across the back of the head.

Chest: Measure around the back and across the chest, just under the armpits (with the baby's arms straight out to the sides).

Belly: Measure around the fullest part of the stomach.

Length: Measure from the top of the head to the heel.

Outseam: Measure from the waist or top of the pants down the outside seam to the ankle.

Inseam: Measure a pair of pants from the crotch to the hem.

Foot length: Measure from the back edge of the heel to the tip of the big toe.

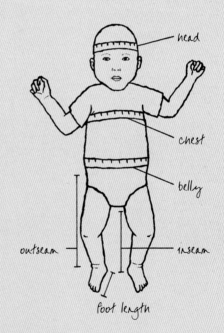

basic tools

- Chalk pencil
- Fabric marker
- Iron
- Ironing board
- Ruler
- Scissors
- Straight pins
- Tape measure
- Turning tool (such as a closed pair of scissors)

general notes for all projects

- Be sure to have the basic tools on hand before beginning a project. See Basic Tools list above for all projects.

- See Fabric Reference Guide (page 173) for a list of the specific fabrics used in each project.

- The first time a term is mentioned and followed by an asterisk (*), it is defined in Glossary and Techniques (page 169).

- Preshrink fabric by washing, drying, and pressing it before starting the project.

- All seams are ½" unless otherwise stated. (The ½" seam allowance is included in the pattern pieces and all cutting measurements.)

- To cut a pattern piece on the fold, lay it even with the folded edge of the fabric. Once the fabric piece is cut out, open it up to yield one full-size panel.

chapter: 2.0 baby comforts

* SNUGGIE WRAP BLANKET * MODERN CRIB SET WITH STORAGE POCKETS * BED BUGS * KIMONO-STYLE PJs

Sweet dreams start with soft surroundings and comfy, warm nests. A most snuggly wrap blanket and a very mod crib set are accompanied by some friendly bed bugs to cuddle and a kimono-style PJ set (for the baby of leisure). These creature comforts—and a kiss on the forehead—will help send baby to sweet dreamland.

a.

SNUGGIE WRAP BLANKET ⇒   instructions: _P.26

DIFFICULTY LEVEL 2

DIFFICULTY LEVEL ❄ 3

MODERN CRIB SET WITH STORAGE POCKETS ⟹

instructions: P.30

C.

3 DIFFICULTY LEVEL

BED BUGS ⇒

instructions: *P.38*

KIMONO-STYLE PJs ⇒   instructions: ___P.43

DIFFICULTY LEVEL 3

a.

snuggie wrap blanket

finished size: 28" x 28" (0–3 months) or 32" x 32" (3–6 months)
difficulty level: 2

Baby will be cozy in modern origami style. A corner hoodie keeps baby's head warm, while the blanket wraps as loose or snug as you want, with a simple, adjustable tie closure. It's easy to make and easy to clean.

FABRICS

For size 0–3 months

* 1 ⅝ yards (44" wide) mid-weight fabric for the exterior and tie

* ⅞ yard (54" wide) fleece for the front and hood lining

For size 3–6 months

* 1 ¾ yards (44" wide) mid-weight fabric for the exterior and tie

* 1 yard (54" wide) fleece for the front and hood lining

OTHER SUPPLIES

* 1 yard lightweight fusible fleece (optional; see Notes)

* 1 spool coordinating all-purpose thread (we use Coats Dual Duty Plus)

* Small dinner plate or cereal bowl (to mark curved edge)

NOTES

* For a heavier, winter Snuggie, add a lightweight fusible fleece to the back panel before sewing it to the front.

* Be careful not to stretch the fleece while cutting or sewing it.

• STEP 1 •

Cut out all of the pieces from the fabric.

Measure and mark the dimensions on the Right side of the fabric. Cut along the marked lines.

a. From the exterior fabric, cut:

Size 0–3

- 1 back panel, 29" wide x 29" long
- 2 tie strips, each 4" wide x 22 ½" long
- 2 short border strips, each 3 ½" wide x 24" long
- 2 long border strips, each 3 ½" wide x 29" long
- 1 hood exterior, 11 ½" wide x 11 ½" long

Size 3–6

- 1 back panel, 33" wide x 33" long
- 2 tie strips, each 4" wide x 22 ½" long
- 2 short border strips, each 3 ½" wide x 28" long
- 2 long border strips, each 3 ½" wide x 33" long
- 1 hood exterior, 11 ½" wide x 11 ½" long

b. From the fleece, cut:

Size 0–3

- 1 front panel, 29" wide x 29" long
- 1 hood lining, 11 ½" wide x 11 ½" long

Size 3–6

- 1 front panel, 33" wide x 33" long
- 1 hood lining, 11 ½" wide x 11 ½" long

c. Optional: If making the heavier, winter Snuggie, from the lightweight fusible fleece, cut:

Size 0–3

- 1 panel, 29" wide x 29" long

Size 3–6

- 1 panel, 33" wide x 33" long

• STEP 2 •

Sew the border to the fleece. (FIGURE 1)

a. With the Right sides together, center one short border strip on the fleece front panel, 2 ½" from the fleece's edge. Pin in place.

b. Stitch a ½" seam along the outside edge of the border, backstitching* at each end.

c. Fold the border back to the edge of the fleece, with the Wrong side of the fabric to the Right side of the fleece. Press at a low temperature.

d. Repeat, first attaching the second short strip to the opposite edge of the fleece, then attaching the long border strips to the remaining two edges.

e. Machine baste* all around the piece, sewing the outside edge of the borders to the fleece.

• STEP 3 •

Make the hood.

a. Fold the hood lining diagonally into a triangle. Gently press a crease along the fold and then open the fabric. Cut along the bias* crease to create a triangle measuring 11 ½" x 11 ½" x 16 ¼". (You will use only one of the triangle pieces.)

b. Fold and cut the hood exterior in the same way.

c. Place the exterior and lining Right sides together. Pin the long edge. Sew a ½" seam along the long edge, backstitching at each end. Turn the hood Right side out, and press at a low temperature. Topstitch* ½" from the stitched edge.

d. Machine baste the remaining two edges.

• STEP 4 •

Attach the hood, and shape the corner.

a. Place the hood in one corner, fleece sides together. Pin it in place.

b. The corner with the hood will be curved. To make a neat arc, measure and mark 4" out from the corner along each edge. Place the dinner plate upside down on top of the hood, matching the edges of the plate to the marks. Use a fabric marker to draw along the top edge of the plate from mark to mark. Cut along the marked line through all layers. Machine baste the edges.

• STEP 5 •

Sew the front and back together. (FIGURE 2)

note: If making the heavier, winter Snuggie, place the Wrong side of the back panel on the fusible side of the lightweight fleece. Follow the manufacturer's instructions to fuse the two layers together using an iron's "wool" setting. Continue with the instructions to complete the Snuggie.

a. Place the front and back panels Right sides together, matching all raw edges. Pin them in place. Trim the back panel to match the front at the hood's rounded corner.

b. Stitch a ½" seam around the outer edges, leaving an 8" opening centered along one side, backstitching at each end.

c. Trim the extra fabric from the corners, leaving a ½" seam allowance*.

d. Turn the Snuggie Right side out. Turn the hood so the fleece lining is facing the fleece front. Using a turning tool*, push out the corners and smooth the hood's rounded seam. Press the edges at a low temperature.

e. Fold each edge ½" under along the opening, and pin them together. Slipstitch* the opening closed. Topstitch a ½" seam around all four edges, lifting up the hood and stitching around the edges, backstitching at each end.

f. Topstitch around all four sides on the fleece close to the seam that attaches the fleece and border strips.

Make buttonholes* for the tie. (FIGURE 2)

a. Fold the Snuggie in half so it forms a triangle with the hood on one of the folded corners. Gently press a crease at the fold, then open the panel.

b. Measure down the center crease from the top corner of the hood. For size 0–3 months, measure 15 ½". For size 3–6 months, measure 17 ½". Use a fabric marker to make two marks ¾" on each side of the center crease, to indicate where the tops of the buttonholes should be. Make two 2" buttonholes on each side of the center crease. The buttonholes are larger than the tie, so as your baby grows you can move the tie down in the buttonholes to allow it to wrap around your baby's tummy.

Make and insert the tie. (FIGURE 2)

a. Place the tie strips Right sides together matching one short end. Pin in place. Stitch a ½" seam along the pinned edge, backstitching at each end. Press the seam allowance open.

b. To make the tie, follow the directions for making a strap (see page 172), with one additional step: After folding the long edges in to meet the center crease, fold each of the short ends ¼" toward the Wrong side and press. Then fold each of the four corners into the center crease to create a point on each end of the tie. Continue with the instructions to complete the tie.

c. On the back of the Snuggie, thread the tie through the buttonholes, centering it in place.

Bundle baby in the Snuggie Wrap Blanket.

a. Place baby in the center of the Snuggie on his/her back, with his/her head in the hood.

b. Fold the bottom flap of the Snuggie up over baby's legs and body.

c. Fold the right flap of the Snuggie over baby's body, tucking the point under baby's left side. Fold the left flap over the right flap, tucking the point underneath the wrapped baby.

d. Tie it snugly, but not too tight, around baby's middle.

Figure 1.

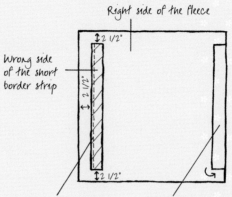

Right side of the fleece

Wrong side of the short border strip

2 1/2"

2 1/2"

2 1/2"

Place strip 2 1/2" from edge of the fleece. Stitch 1/2" from outside edge of strip.

Right side of the short edge strip, folded back to edge of the fleece. Press.

Figure 2.

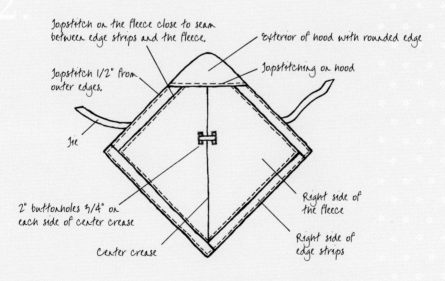

Topstitch on the fleece close to seam between edge strips and the fleece.

Exterior of hood with rounded edge

Topstitch 1/2" from outer edges.

Topstitching on hood

Tie

2" buttonholes 3/4" on each side of center crease

Center crease

Right side of the fleece

Right side of edge strips

b.

modern crib set WITH STORAGE POCKETS

pillow sham finished size: 12" wide x 16" long

fitted sheet finished size: 28" wide x 52" long x 8" deep (fits a standard crib mattress)

reversible tied quilt finished size: 36" wide x 50" long

crib skirt finished size: 28" wide x 52" long x 15" from deck to hem (see Note)

crib bumper finished size: 10" wide x 160" long (fits a standard crib)

difficulty level: 3

Customize baby's room with this clean-lined crib set that looks as good as it works. The fitted sheet, bumper pad with pockets for holding books and toys, pillow cover and bed skirt, and a beautiful quilted comforter will complement any decor. Always take care that items placed inside the crib do not compromise safe sleeping positions for baby.

FABRICS

For Pillow Sham

* ½ yard (44" or 54" wide) mid-weight print for the pillow's front

* ½ yard (44" or 54" wide) coordinating mid-weight print for the pillow's back

* ½ yard (44" wide) muslin to line the pillow's front

For Fitted Sheet

* 3 ½ yards (44" wide) mid-weight fabric or 2 yards (54" wide) mid-weight fabric

For Reversible Tied Quilt

* 1 ½ yards (44" or 54" wide) mid-weight print for the front panel

* 1 ⅝ yards (44" or 54" wide) second mid-weight print for the back panel

* ⅝ yard (44" or 54" wide) third mid-weight print for the binding

For Crib Skirt

* 1 ⅝ yards (44" or 54" wide) muslin for the deck. Note: The deck is the hidden part of the crib skirt under the mattress.

* 3 yards (44" or 54" wide) mid-weight print for the skirt panels

For Crib Bumper

* 2 yards (44" or 54" wide) mid-weight fabric for the exterior and ties

* 4 ½ yards (44" or 54" wide) coordinating mid-weight fabric for the interior and pockets

OTHER SUPPLIES

For Pillow Sham

* ¾ yard (20" wide) mid-weight woven fusible interfacing (we use SF101 by Pellon)

* ⅜ yard (44" wide) fusible fleece (we use Fusible Thermolam Plus by Pellon)

* 1 spool coordinating all-purpose thread (we use Coats Dual Duty Plus)

* 12" x 16" pillow form (we use Soft Touch by Fairfield)

For Fitted Sheet

* 1 spool coordinating all-purpose thread (we use Coats Dual Duty Plus)

* 1 ¼ yards of ¼" wide elastic

* Medium-size safety pin

For Reversible Tied Quilt

* 2 packages Poly-fil Hi-Loft Batting by Fairfield, crib size (45" x 60")

* Masking tape (optional)

* 1 spool coordinating all-purpose thread (we use Coats Dual Duty Plus)

* 1 skein coordinating perle cotton embroidery floss for tying the quilt

* Tapestry needle (size 20 or 22)

* Walking foot or even-feed foot for sewing machine (optional but extremely helpful)

For Crib Skirt

* 1 spool coordinating all-purpose thread (we use Coats Dual Duty Plus)

For Crib Bumper

* 1 ⅝ yards (20" wide) mid-weight woven fusible interfacing (we use SF101 by Pellon)

* 1 spool coordinating all-purpose thread (we use Coats Dual Duty Plus)

* 1 package Nu-Foam Bumper Pads by Fairfield

* Hand-sewing needle

pillow sham

• STEP 1 •
Cut out all of the pieces from the fabric.

From the first print, cut:

- 1 front panel, 17" wide x 13" long

From the second print, cut:

- 2 back panels, each 11 ¼" wide x 13" long

From the muslin, cut:

- 1 lining panel, 17" wide x 13" long

From the fusible interfacing, cut:

- 2 panels, each 11 ¼" wide x 13" long

From the fusible fleece, cut:

- 1 panel, 17" wide x 13" long

• STEP 2 •
Prepare and make the pillow's back.

a. Place the first back panel Right side up on the interfacing's fusible side. Follow the manufacturer's instructions to fuse them together, using an iron's "wool" setting.

b. Repeat to fuse interfacing to the second back panel.

c. Place one of the back panels Wrong side up. Fold one long end over (Wrong sides together) by ½", and press in place. Turn the same edge over again in the same direction, this time by 1". Press. Pin the folded end in place. Stitch a seam along the pinned edge, close to the first folded edge. Backstitch* at each end.

d. Repeat to finish one long edge of the second back panel.

e. Place the two back panels so their finished edges overlap by 2 ½". Pin them together. Machine baste* across the top and bottom raw edges.

• STEP 3 •
Prepare and make the pillow's front.

a. Place the muslin on the fusible side of the fleece. Follow the manufacturer's instructions to fuse them together, using an iron's "wool" setting.

b. Place the Wrong side of the front panel toward the fleece side of the muslin panel matching the raw edges, and pin them together. Then machine baste completely around the outer edges.

• STEP 4 •
Complete the pillow.

a. Pin the completed front to the back panels, Right sides together, matching all the edges. Stitch a ½" seam completely around the pinned edges, and backstitch at each end. Trim the seam allowance* to ¼". Zigzag or serge around the seam allowance.

b. Turn the pillow Right side out. Push out the corners using a turning tool*.

c. Insert the pillow form through the opening in the back.

fitted sheet

⟹ IF USING 44"-WIDE FABRIC:

• STEP 1 •

Cut from the fabric:

- 1 center panel, 29" wide x 69 ½" long
- 2 side panels, each 9 ¼" wide x 52" long

• STEP 2 •

Make the sheet.

a. Find the center of all three panels by folding each in half, matching the short edges. Gently press the creases at the folds.

b. Place the side panels on each side of the center panel, Right sides together, matching the panels at the creases. Pin the long edges. Starting and stopping ½" in from each end of the side panels, stitch a ½" seam along the pinned edges.

c. On the center panel, clip* into the seam allowance at each end of the stitching line. Be careful not to cut the stitching.

d. Keeping the Right sides together, turn the center panel at the clip to meet the side panel's first short end. Pin them in place. Stitch a ½" seam along the pinned edge to create a corner. Repeat to make the remaining three corners.

e. Zigzag or serge along the raw edges of the seam allowances. Trim any extra fabric.

f. At the bottom edges, turn ¼" of fabric toward the Wrong side all the way around. Press this fold. Turn it under again, this time by ½", toward the Wrong side. Press, and pin it in place.

g. Measure 8" out from the corner seam on one long side's edge. Make a mark at the 8" point. Repeat to mark at the remaining three corners.

h. Edge stitch* along the inner folded edge completely around the bottom edge, leaving a 1" opening at each of the four marks on the long side edges. Backstitch at each end.

• STEP 3 •

Add elastic to the sheet's short ends. (FIGURE 1)

a. Cut the elastic in half to make two pieces, each 22" long. Attach the safety pin on one end of the first length of the elastic. Insert the pin with the elastic in one of the 1" openings you left in Step 2h. Thread the safety pin through the folded edge, across the short end of the sheet, and out through the opening on the opposite side.

b. Stitch through the elastic at each end, at the openings, to hold the elastic in place.

c. Repeat to insert the remaining piece of elastic around the sheet's other short end.

d. Stitch all four openings closed, backstitching at each end.

⟹ IF USING 54"-WIDE FABRIC:

• STEP 1 •

Cut from the fabric:

- 1 panel, 45 ½" wide x 69 ½" long

• STEP 2 •

Make the sheet.

a. Cut an 8 ¾" square from each corner of the panel.

b. On one corner, place the cut edges Right sides together. Pin them together. Stitch a ½" seam along the pinned edge. Zigzag or serge along the seam allowance's raw edges.

c. Repeat to make the three remaining corners.

d. Turn the bottom edges under following the instructions in step 2f through 2h, and insert the elastic as instructed in step 3 for 44"-wide fabric.

Figure 1.

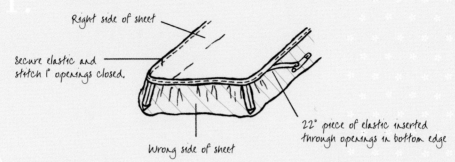

Right side of sheet

Secure elastic and
stitch 1" openings closed.

22" piece of elastic inserted
through openings in bottom edge

Wrong side of sheet

reversible tied quilt

• STEP 1 •

Cut out all of the pieces from the fabric.

From the first fabric, cut:

- 1 front panel, 36" wide x 50" long

From the second fabric, cut:

- 1 back panel, 40" wide x 54" long

From the third fabric, cut:

- 190" (3 ½" wide) of French straight binding*

• STEP 2 •

Prepare the quilt's layers.

a. Remove the batting from the packages. Unfold it and set it aside, allowing the wrinkles to flatten.

b. Place the back panel on a large, flat surface Wrong side up. Smooth out any wrinkles (press the panel, if needed). You may find it helpful to tape its edges to the surface to keep it in place while you assemble the quilt.

c. Place both layers of batting on top of the back panel. Smooth out any wrinkles. Trim the edges of batting so they are even with the back panel.

d. Place the front panel Right side up on top of the batting. Center the front panel on the batting and the back panel. Pin the layers together, pinning all over the quilt (especially along the edges).

• STEP 3 •

Prepare the binding, and attach it to the quilt.

a. Prepare French straight binding as instructed in Glossary and Techniques (page 170). If possible, use a sewing machine's walking foot or even-feed foot to apply the binding to the Right side of the front panel.

b. Trim the back panel and batting even with the edge of the front panel and the binding. Turn the binding to the back and pin it in place. Then slipstitch* around the edge of the binding.

• STEP 4 •

Mark and tie the quilt. (FIGURE 2)

a. Starting in the middle of the quilt, use a fabric marker to make rows of marks 6" apart. Offset each row from the one above and below it, so the marks form diamond shapes:

x x x x x x

x x x x x

x x x x x x

b. Use a tapestry needle and perle cotton embroidery floss to create the ties. Insert the needle through a mark on the front, pushing straight through to the back. Bring the needle back up through all the layers of the quilt, making a small stitch on the back. Cut the floss, leaving 4" tails of thread. Repeat at each mark.

c. Tie the tails of each stitch in a double knot. Trim the tails to ½" to 1" long.

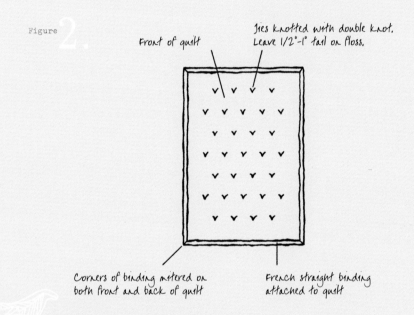

Figure 2.

Front of quilt

Ties knotted with double knot. Leave 1/2"-1" tail on floss.

Corners of binding mitered on both front and back of quilt

French straight binding attached to quilt

crib skirt

• STEP 1 •

Cut out all of the pieces from the fabric.

For the deck, cut from the muslin:

- 1 panel, 29" wide x 53" long

For the skirt, cut from the printed fabric:

- 2 end panels, each 30" wide x 16 ½" long
- 4 side panels, each 29" wide x 16 ½" long
- 2 side inserts, each 8" wide x 16 ½" long

• STEP 2 •

Hem the bottoms of the skirt panels.

a. Fold ½" under toward the Wrong side on the bottom edge of the first end panel, and press. Fold this edge ½" under again, and press. Pin the folded edge in place. Edge stitch close to the inner folded edge and backstitch at each end.

b. Repeat to hem the second end panel, four side panels, and the short, bottom edges of both side inserts.

Hem the sides of the skirt panels.

a. On each short side of the first end panel, fold the edge under ½" toward the Wrong side, and press. Fold it under again ½" toward the Wrong side. Press, and pin it in place. Stitch along the inner folded edge and backstitch at each end.

b. Repeat to hem both sides of the second end panel, and the long side edges of both side inserts.

c. Turn each side panel under by 1" along the center sides, toward the Wrong side. Press. Repeat, again turning 1" toward the Wrong side. Press, and pin in place. Stitch along the inner pinned edge and backstitch at each end.

d. Turn each side panel's outer sides under ½" toward the Wrong side. Press. Repeat, again turning ½" toward the Wrong side. Press, and pin in place. Stitch along the inner pinned edge and backstitch at each end.

Attach the skirt panels to the deck. (FIGURE 3)

a. Fold the deck in half, matching the short ends. Gently press a crease on the fold.

b. Fold the side inserts in half, matching the long edges. Gently press a crease on the fold of each one.

c. Center and pin the raw edge of the first end panel to the one short end of the deck, Right sides together. Stitch a ½" seam along the pinned edge and backstitch at each end.

d. Repeat to attach the second end panel to the deck's opposite short end.

e. Pin two side panels to one long edge of the deck, Right sides together. Match the center finished edge to the deck's center crease. Pin the Right side of the first side insert to the Wrong side of the side panels, matching the center crease of the side insert to the center crease of the deck. Stitch a ½" seam along the pinned edge, stitching through the deck, side panels, and side insert. Backstitch at each end.

f. Repeat to attach the second set of side panels and the second side insert to the deck's other long edge.

g. Zigzag or serge along the seam allowances. Press the seam allowances toward the deck, then pin them in place. Edge stitch the seam allowances to the deck.

Figure

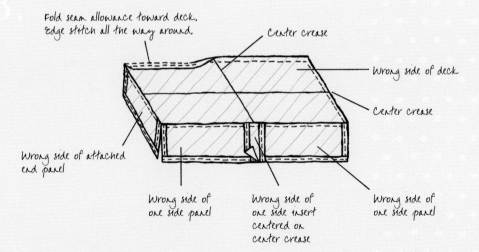

Fold seam allowance toward deck. Edge stitch all the way around.

Center crease

Wrong side of deck

Center crease

Wrong side of attached end panel

Wrong side of one side panel

Wrong side of one side insert centered on center crease

Wrong side of one side panel

crib bumper with pockets

• STEP 1 •

Cut out all of the pieces from the fabric.

From the first fabric, cut:

- 6 exterior panels, each 27 ½" wide x 11 ¾" long
- 12 ties, each 2" wide x 22" long
- 2 tie loops, each 2" wide x 2 ¾" long

From the second fabric, cut:

- 8 pocket panels, each 27 ½" wide x 10" long
- 6 interior panels, each 27 ½" wide x 11 ¾" long

From the fusible interfacing, cut:

- 4 panels, each 27 ½" wide x 10" long

• STEP 2 •

Fuse interfacing to the pocket panels.

a. Place one pocket panel Right side up on the interfacing's fusible side. Follow the manufacturer's instructions to fuse them together, using an iron's "wool" setting.

b. Repeat with three additional pocket panels.

• STEP 3 •

Make the pockets.

a. With Right sides together, pin one pocket panel (with interfacing) and one pocket panel (without interfacing) along the top long edge. Stitch a ½" seam along the pinned edge and backstitch* at each end.

b. Turn the pocket panels Right side out. Press. Stitch a ½" seam along the top finished edge.

c. Pin and machine baste* the remaining edges.

d. Repeat Steps 3a through 3c to make three more pockets.

e. Pin the first complete pocket to one interior panel, Right sides together, matching side and bottom raw edges. Machine baste along the side and bottom edges.

f. Repeat to attach the remaining three pockets to three interior panels.

• STEP 4 •

Attach the interior panels.

a. Pin the interior panels together at their short ends, Right sides together, in the following sequence, making one long piece:

1. Interior panel without pocket
2. Interior panel with pocket
3. Interior panel with pocket
4. Interior panel without pocket
5. Interior panel with pocket
6. Interior panel with pocket

b. Sew them together with ½" seams, backstitching at each end. Press the seam allowances* open.

• STEP 5 •

Attach the exterior panels.

a. Pin the exterior panels together at their short ends, Right sides together, to make one long piece.

b. Sew them together with ½" seams, backstitching at each end. Press the seam allowances open.

• STEP 6 •

Make the ties and tie loops.

a. Turn under ½" on each tie's short end, toward the Wrong side, and press. Make 12 ties (see page 172). Set them aside.

b. Make two loops using the same technique as for the ties, but do not turn under the ends.

• STEP 7 •

Attach the loops, and then join the exterior and interior panels. (FIGURE 4)

a. Fold the loops in half, matching the short ends. Pin the loops to the Right side of one interior panel without pockets; place one ¾" from the top along the side edge, and the other ¾" from the bottom, also on the side edge. Match the short ends of the loops to the raw edge of the interior panel.

b. Pin the exterior panels to the interior panels, Right sides together, matching the seams and raw edges.

c. Along the bottom edge, measure in 6" from the bottom corners and use a fabric marker to make marks.

d. At each seam, measure 6" out in both directions along the bottom edge and make marks.

e. Begin stitching a ½" seam at the first 6" mark (at one bottom corner). Stitch to the corner, up the short edge, across the long top edge, down the opposite short edge, and to the first 6" mark at the opposite end of the bottom. Backstitch at each end.

f. At each seam on the bottom edge, stitch a ½" seam between the 6" marks, making a 12"-long seam with 14 ½" openings at the bottom of each panel.

g. Trim the corners and turn the attached panels Right side out, using a turning tool* to push out the corners. Press the panels.

h. Match the seams between the exterior and interior panels and pin them in place. Stitch-in-the-ditch* along each seam, backstitching at each end.

· STEP 8 ·

Attach the ties. (FIGURE 5)

a. Find the center of each tie by folding it in half, matching the short ends. Gently press a crease at the fold.

b. Pin the ties to the exterior's top and bottom edges, centering the ties' creases on the seams. Place them on the exterior, at the center and each end of the pocket panels.

c. Stitch through each tie, following the seam line. Backstitch at each end.

· STEP 9 ·

Insert the pads, and complete the bumper.

a. Insert one foam pad through each opening along the bottom edge. Push the foam into the cover's corners.

b. Fold the seam allowance under ½" on each side of the open edges. Pin the edges together, and then slipstitch* them closed.

Figure 4

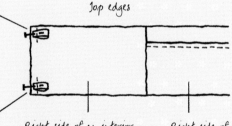

Place the first loop, folded in half, on the side edge 3/4" down from the top edge. Pin and then machine baste it in place.

Place the second loop on the side edge 3/4" up from the bottom edge. Pin and machine baste it in place.

Top edges

Right side of an interior panel without a pocket

Right side of an interior panel with a pocket

Figure 5

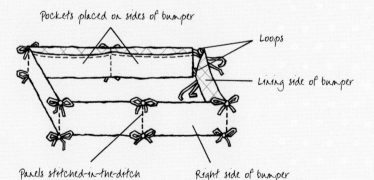

Pockets placed on sides of bumper

Loops

Lining side of bumper

Right side of bumper

Panels stitched-in-the-ditch

C.

BED BUGS

ladybugs finished size: small: 4 ½" wide x 6" long x 2" high; large: 5 ½" wide x 8 ½" long x 3" high
butterflies finished size: small: 9" wide x 6" long x 2" high; large: 11 ½" wide x 8" long x 3" high
difficulty level: 3

Soft and comforting buddies for bedtime, the butterfly and ladybug come in two sizes and contain soft-sounding rattles to entertain and soothe the little sleeper. Create your own mix of great prints for funky or subtly snug bugs.

FABRICS

For small Ladybug

* ¼ yard (44" or 54" wide) mid-weight print for the body and belly

* ⅛ yard (44" or 54" wide) mid-weight solid fabric for the spots, stripe, head, and antennae

* ¼ yard (44" wide) fusible fleece (we use Fusible Thermolam Plus by Pellon)

For large Ladybug

* ⅜ yard (44" or 54" wide) mid-weight print for the body and belly

* ⅛ yard (44" or 54" wide) mid-weight solid fabric for the spots, stripe, head, and antennae

* ⅜ yard (44" wide) fusible fleece (we use Fusible Thermolam Plus by Pellon)

For small Butterfly

* 8" x 8" scrap mid-weight solid for the body and spots

* ¼ yard (44" or 54" wide) mid-weight print for the wings and antennae

For large Butterfly

* 10" x 10" scrap mid-weight solid for the body and spots

* ⅜ yard (44" or 54" wide) mid-weight print for the wings and antennae

OTHER SUPPLIES

For Ladybug

* ¼ yard (17" wide) Wonder-Under or similar fusible webbing

* Tracing wheel and tracing paper

* 1 spool coordinating all-purpose thread (we use Coats Dual Duty Plus)

* 1 bag (12 oz.) Nature-fil (all-natural premium fiberfill by Fairfield)

* 12 size-20 mm jingle bells (such as Jingle Bell from Fiber-Craft Materials Corporation)

* Sharp hand-sewing needle

For small Butterfly

* 4" x 4" piece of Wonder-Under or similar fusible webbing

* Wax-free tracing paper by Prym-Dritz

* Tracing wheel

* 1 spool coordinating all-purpose thread (we use Coats Dual Duty Plus)

* 1 bag (12 oz.) of Nature-fil (all-natural premium fiberfill by Fairfield)

* 6 size-16 mm jingle bells (such as Jingle Bell by Fiber-Craft Materials Corporation)

For large Butterfly

* 4" x 4" piece of Wonder-Under or similar fusible webbing

* 1 spool coordinating all-purpose thread (we use Coats Dual Duty Plus)

* 1 bag (12 oz.) Nature-fil (all-natural premium fiberfill by Fairfield)

* 6 size-20 mm jingle bells (such as Jingle Bell by Fiber-Craft Materials Corporation)

NOTE

* One bag of Nature-fil is enough to make all four Bed Bugs.

ladybugs

FOLLOW INSTRUCTIONS BELOW FOR EITHER SIZE LADYBUG.

• STEP 1 •

Cut out the ladybug pieces from the pattern sheet included with this book.

Cut out the pattern pieces for the size ladybug you are making:

- Body
- Spots
- Belly
- Head

• STEP 2 •

Cut out all of the pieces from the fabric.

a. Fold the fabric in half lengthwise with the Wrong sides together, and press a center crease. Open the fabric. Fold each selvage edge* in to meet the center crease and gently press along each folded edge.

b. From the print, cut (see General Notes, page 13):

- 1 body on the fold
- 1 belly on the fold

c. From the solid fabric, cut:

- 1 antenna (for small ladybug: 1 ¼" wide x 6" long; for large ladybug: 1 ½" wide x 7" long)

d. Place the web side of the Wonder-Under onto the Wrong side of the remaining solid fabric and fuse following the manufacturer's instructions. Trace the pattern pieces on the Right side of the fabric.

From the fused solid fabric with Wonder-Under, cut:

- 1 head on the fold
- 2 small spots (for small ladybug: 1 ¼" spots; for large ladybug: 1 ½" spots)
- 2 large spots (for small ladybug: 1 ⅝" spots; for large ladybug: 1 ⅞" spots)
- 1 stripe (for small ladybug: ⅜" wide x 5 ⅛" long; for large ladybug: ½" wide x 6 ⅛" long)

e. From the fusible fleece, cut:

- 1 body on the fold

• STEP 3 •

Transfer the lines* and marks* from the pattern piece to the ladybug body.

Use tracing paper*, a tracing wheel* or a chalk pencil, and the pattern piece as a guide.

- Transfer the lines for the spots, head, and stripe onto the Right side of the ladybug body.
- Transfer the antennae's placement marks onto the Right side of the ladybug head.

• STEP 4 •

Make the antennae.

a. Fold the antennae piece in half lengthwise, Wrong sides together, and press a crease along the fold. Open up the fabric. Fold each long edge in so it touches the center crease, and press again. Fold ¼" in on each short end of the antennae and press. Fold lengthwise along the center crease to enclose the raw edges. Edge stitch* down both sides, backstitching* at each end.

b. Tie a knot at each end of the antennae piece. Push the knot to the end and pull it tight.

c. Fold the antennae piece in half, matching the knots. Cut it in half at the fold to make two antennae. Set it aside.

• STEP 5 •

Attach the spots, stripe, head, and antennae to the ladybug body.

a. Remove the paper backing from the spots, stripe, and head. Place each spot within the placement lines on the body. Place one end of the stripe ¼" past the placement line for the head, and place the head inside the lines on top of the stripe. Fuse all the details to the body, following the manufacturer's instructions.

b. Machine satin stitch in a tight zigzag completely around each spot, around the inside edges of the head, and down both sides of the stripe, backstitching at each end.

c. Place the Wrong side of the body on top of the fusible side of the fleece. Use a pressing cloth* and follow the manufacturer's instruction to fuse.

d. Place the cut end of each antenna to the inside of the placement marks on the ladybug head, matching the raw edges. The antennae should be lying on the head, not sticking out. Pin the antennae in place, and machine baste* across their ends to hold them in place while you finish the body.

• STEP 6 •

Make the ladybug body. (FIGURE 1)

a. Fold the body in half lengthwise, then fold it again widthwise. Press about 1" in on each folded edge to mark the body into quarters. Unfold the body.

b. Repeat to mark the belly into quarters.

c. Sew a ½" gathering stitch* completely around the body, then slightly pull the bobbin thread. Place the body and belly Right sides together, matching each quarter crease and tucking the antennae inside. Evenly gather the body to fit the belly. Pin the pieces together. Stitch a ½" seam around the body, leaving a 3" opening on the bottom of the ladybug, and backstitch at each end.

d. Trim the seam allowance* to ¼". Clip* into the seam allowance every ½" to ¾" all the way around the ladybug.

• STEP 7 •

Stuff the ladybug.

a. Turn the ladybug Right side out, pushing out the edges, and press. Stuff the body firmly with fiberfill.

b. Make a packet for the bells by folding a 4" x 4" scrap of fabric in half and stitching a ¼" seam along two edges, leaving one end open. Insert 6 bells. Stitch the opening closed, and trim any excess fabric.

c. Using your fingers, make a small hole in the ladybug's stuffing. Insert the packet of bells, and close the fiberfill around it.

d. Fold under the raw edges of the opening by ½". Pin, and then slipstitch* the opening closed.

Figure

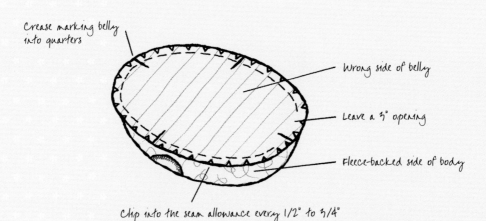

Crease marking belly into quarters

Wrong side of belly

Leave a 3" opening

Fleece-backed side of body

Clip into the seam allowance every 1/2" to 3/4"

butterflies

• STEP 1 •

Cut out the butterfly pieces from the pattern sheet included with this book.

Cut out the pattern pieces for the size butterfly you are making:

- Wings
- Spots
- Body

• STEP 2 •

Cut out all of the pieces from the fabric.

a. Fold the fabric in half lengthwise Wrong sides together, matching the selvage edges*.

b. From the solid fabric, cut:

- 2 bodies

c. Place the web side of the Wonder-Under on the Wrong side of the remaining scrap of the solid fabric and fuse following the manufacturer's instructions.

From the fused solid fabric and Wonder-Under, cut:

- 2 spots for the top of the wing (for small butterfly: 1 ½" spots; for large butterfly: 1 ⅞" spots)
- 2 spots for the bottom of the wing (for small butterfly: 1 ¼" spots; for large butterfly: 1 ⅝" spots)

From the printed fabric, cut:

- 4 wings
- 1 antenna (for small butterfly: 1" wide x 6" long; for large butterfly: 1" wide x 7" long)

• STEP 3 •

Transfer the lines* and marks* from the pattern piece to the butterfly pieces.

a. Use tracing paper*, a tracing wheel* or a chalk pencil, and the pattern piece as a guide.

- Transfer the lines for the spots on the top and bottom of one wing. Then flip the pattern piece over so the writing side is facing the Right side of a second wing and trace the spots on the top and bottom of it.

- Transfer the marks for the antennae placement to the top of one body.
- Transfer the stitching line onto the Wrong side of one set of wings.

• STEP 4 •

Attach the spots to the wings. (FIGURE 2)

a. Remove the paper backing from each spot.

b. Place the spots within the placement lines at the top and bottom of the first wing. Fuse in place following the manufacturer's instructions. Machine satin stitch in a tight zigzag completely around each spot.

c. Repeat to attach two other spots to the second marked wing.

• STEP 5 •

Make the antennae, and attach them to the body. (FIGURE 2)

a. Follow the ladybug antennae instructions on page 39, Step 4, to make 2 antennae for the butterfly.

b. On the Right side at the top of the body, place the raw end of each antenna inside its placement marks. Pin the antennae in place. (The antennae should be lying on the body.) Machine baste* across the ends of both antennae to hold them in place while you finish the body.

• STEP 6 •

Attach the wings to the body.

a. Fold both butterfly bodies in half, matching the short, rounded edges. Gently press creases to mark the centers of each body.

b. Fold each wing in half, matching the top and bottom edges. Gently press creases to mark the centers of each wing.

c. Place the first wing without spots and the body without antennae Right sides together, matching the center creases on the body and wing. Pin them together. Stitch a ½" seam to attach the wing to the body, backstitching* at each end. Press the seam allowance* toward the wing.

d. Place the second wing without spots Right sides together onto the other side of the body. Match the creases and pin in place. Stitch a ½" seam, 1" in length, at the top and bottom of the wing. (The opening will be used to turn the butterfly Right side out.)

e. Repeat to attach the other set of wings with spots to the body with the antennae. Stitch all the way down the second wing; do not leave an opening.

Attach the front to the back. (FIGURE 3)

a. Place the front and back of the butterfly Right sides together, matching the edges. Pin in place.

b. Stitch a ½" seam around the outside edges of the butterfly, pivoting* at the sharp turns. Backstitch at each end.

c. Clip* into the seam allowance up to the stitching line as shown in Figure 3, making sure not to clip the stitching. It is important to clip into the corners on either side of the head and tail and also at the point at the center of each wing so the butterfly will look better when you turn it Right side out.

Turn the butterfly Right side out and stuff it.

a. Turn the butterfly Right side out. Push out the wings, head, and tail of the body. Press it flat.

b. Insert fiberfill in each wing and a small amount in the body. Do not overstuff.

c. Make a packet for the bells by folding a 4" x 4" scrap of fabric in half and stitching a ¼" seam along two edges, leaving one end open. Insert 3 bells. Stitch the opening closed, and trim any excess fabric. Repeat to make another packet with 3 bells.

d. Use your fingers to make a small opening in the stuffing in one of the butterfly's wings. Insert one packet of bells, and close the fiberfill around it. Repeat to insert the other packet into the other wing.

e. Fold under the raw edges of the opening by ½". Pin, and then slipstitch* the opening closed.

f. Match the front and back seams on each side of the body and pin them together. Stitch-in-the-ditch* between the wings and the body on each side, backstitching at each end.

Figure 2

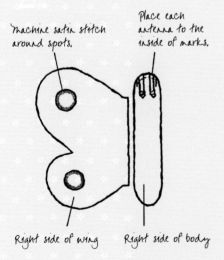

machine satin stitch around spots.

Place each antenna to the inside of marks.

Right side of wing   Right side of body

Figure 3

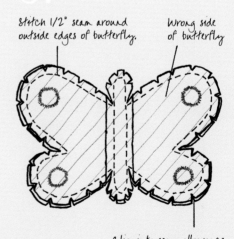

Stitch 1/2" seam around outside edges of butterfly.

Wrong side of butterfly

Clip into seam allowance around curves on wings and top of head and tail.

d.

kimono-style PJs

finished size: 0–3 months, 3–6 months, 6–9 months, 9–12 months
difficulty level: 3

Loose, comfy, and oh-so-stylish for baby, the PJ top has an offset front tie that makes for easy dressing. It can be made with short sleeves, too. The PJ pants have an elastic waist and can be made as shorts.

FABRICS

* 1 yard (44" wide) mid-weight print for sizes 0–3 and 3–6 months; 1 ⅛ yards (44" wide) mid-weight print for sizes 6–9 and 9–12 months

* ½ yard (44" wide) second coordinating mid-weight print for trim on the top and pants and bias binding (for all sizes)

OTHER SUPPLIES

* Medium-size safety pin

* 1 spool coordinating all-purpose thread (we use Coats Dual Duty Plus)

* ⅝ yard (1" wide) non-roll elastic for the waistband

• STEP 1 •

Cut out the pattern pieces.

From the pattern sheet included with this book, cut out:

- Front panel
- Back panel
- Sleeve
- Front pant
- Back pant

• STEP 2 •

Cut out all of the pieces from the fabric.

a. Fold the fabric in half lengthwise, Wrong sides together, matching the selvage edges*.

b. From the first print, cut:

- 2 sleeves on the fold (see General Notes, page 13)
- 1 back panel on the fold
- 2 front panels
- 2 front pants
- 2 back pants

c. Measure and mark the dimensions for the trim directly onto the Right side of the second fabric. Cut along the marked lines.

d. From the second print, cut:

- 2 front trims for the PJ top
  - 0–3 months: 8 ⅛" wide x 3 ½" long
  - 3–6 months: 8 ⅜" wide x 3 ½" long
  - 6–9 months: 8 ⅝" wide x 3 ½" long
  - 9–12 months: 8 ⅞" wide x 3 ½" long

- 1 back trim for the PJ top
  - 0–3 months: 11 ⅞" wide x 3 ½" long
  - 3–6 months: 12 ½" wide x 3 ½" long
  - 6–9 months: 13" wide x 3 ½" long
  - 9–12 months: 13 ¾" wide x 3 ½" long

- 2 front trims for the PJ pants
  - 0–3 or 3–6 months: 6" wide x 3 ½" long
  - 6–9 months: 6 ⅛" wide x 3 ½" long
  - 9–12 months: 6 ¼" wide x 3 ½" long

- 2 back trims for the PJ pants
  - 0–3 or 3–6 months: 7 ¼" wide x 3 ½" long
  - 6–9 months: 7 ⅜" wide x 3 ½" long
  - 9–12 months: 7 ⅜" wide x 3 ½" long

Or, if making shorts, cut:

- 2 front trims for the PJ shorts
  - 0–3 months: 6 ½" wide x 3 ½" long
  - 3–6 months: 6 ¾" wide x 3 ½" long
  - 6–9 months: 6 ⅞" wide x 3 ½" long
  - 9–12 months: 7 ⅛" wide x 3 ½" long

- 2 back trims for the PJ shorts
  - 0–3 months: 7 ⅞" wide x 3 ½" long
  - 3–6 months: 8 ⅛" wide x 3 ½" long
  - 6–9 months: 8 ¼" wide x 3 ½" long
  - 9–12 months: 8 ⅜" wide x 3 ½" long

 note: The bias binding will be cut in Step 4.

e. From the 1" elastic, for pants or shorts, cut:

- 1 waistband
  - 0–3 months: 1 piece, 19" long
  - 3–6 months: 1 piece, 20" long
  - 6–9 months: 1 piece, 21" long
  - 9–12 months: 1 piece, 22" long

---

pj top

FOLLOW INSTRUCTIONS BELOW TO MAKE THE TOP WITH EITHER SHORT OR LONG SLEEVES.

• STEP 3 •

Sew together the front panels, back panel, sleeves, and trim.

a. Place the top edge of the first front trim and bottom edge of one front panel Right sides together, and pin them in place. Stitch them together with a ½" seam, backstitching* at each end. Zigzag or serge the seam allowance*, then press it toward the bottom. Repeat this step to attach the other front panel and the second front trim.

b. Repeat to attach the back trim to the bottom of the back panel.

c. Place one sleeve and one front panel Right sides together at the slanted edge, and pin in place. Stitch a ½" seam along the slanted edge, backstitching at each end. Zigzag or serge the seam allowance, then press it toward the sleeve. Repeat to attach the other top slanted edge of the sleeve to the back panel.

d. Repeat to attach the second sleeve to the other side of the back panel and then to the second front panel. Set aside. (The side seams and hem will be made in steps 6 and 7.)

• STEP 4 •

Make bias binding and ties. Attach the ties to the PJ top.

a. Make 70" of ½"-wide single-fold bias binding from the remaining second fabric (see page 169). Cut binding strips 2" wide.

b. Cut off a 16"-long piece of binding for making the ties. (Set the rest of the binding aside until Step 5.)

c. Open the cut piece of binding. Fold under ½" on each short end toward the Wrong side, and press it down. Fold the binding in half at the center crease, enclosing the raw edges. Edge stitch* down the folded edge of the binding, and backstitch at each end. Then fold the finished piece of binding in half, matching the short ends. Cut along the folded edge to make two pieces of binding for the ties.

d. Place the raw end of one tie 1" down from the sleeve on the Right side of the left front panel. Pin the tie in place. Machine baste* a ½" seam across the end of the tie.

e. Place the raw end of the second tie 1" down from the sleeve on the right front panel, this time on the Wrong side. (This tie will be on the inside of the top when it is completed.) Pin the tie in place. Machine baste across the end of the tie.

• STEP 5 •

Attach the binding to the PJ top. (FIGURE 1)

a. Open up one long edge of the remaining binding. To finish the front edges on the top, place the unfolded edge of the binding and the bottom of the front trim Right sides together, matching the edges. Stop at the slanted edge and pin the binding in place. Cut the binding at the slanted edge on the front of the top. Stitch a ½" seam down the edge, and backstitch at each end.

b. Fold the binding over the top's front edges to the Wrong side, and pin it in place. Edge stitch from the Right side of the front panel, catching the folded edge of the binding on the back, backstitching at each end.

c. Repeat to attach the binding to the other front edge, from the bottom of the trim to the slanted edge.

d. Next, open up one long edge of the remaining binding, and place 7" of the binding hanging free at the start of the slanted edge. (It will be one of the ties when the top is done.) To finish the top edges, place the unfolded edge of the binding Right sides together, matching the edges of the binding up the slanted front, around the neckline, then down the other side, and leaving 7" hanging free past the other front edge. Cut off any excess binding. Pin the binding in place. Stitch a ½" seam around the pinned edges, and backstitch at each end.

e. With the binding opened at the center crease, fold each short end of the binding ½" in toward the Wrong side, and press.

f. Fold the binding over the raw edge to the Wrong side of the PJ top. Place the folded edge of the binding just covering the stitching showing through, and pin it in place. Continue folding at the center crease on the binding left hanging off each end, and pin the edges together. Edge stitch from the Right side of the top, starting at one end of the binding along the matched edges, around the top, and across the binding hanging off the other side, backstitching at each end.

• STEP 6 •

Attach the front and back of the top.

a. Place the top's front and back Right sides together, matching the seam that attaches the sleeve, and pin in place. Stitch a ½" seam from the top's bottom edge to the seam that attaches the sleeve. Pivot* at the seam, then continue stitching to the end of the sleeve, backstitching at each end.

b. Clip* into the seam allowance at the seam that attaches the sleeve, making sure not to clip the stitching. Zigzag or serge the seam allowance, then press it toward the back.

c. Repeat to attach the other side edges and the sleeve together.

• STEP 7 •

Hem the PJ top.

a. Fold the bottom of the trim in by ½", toward the Wrong side, and press. Fold the edge in again ½", and press. Pin it in place.

b. Edge stitch along the inner folded edge, backstitching at each end.

c. Fold the end of the first sleeve in ½", toward the Wrong side, and press. Fold it in ½" again, and press. Pin it in place.

d. Edge stitch along the inner folded edge, backstitching at each end.

e. Repeat to hem the other sleeve.

f. Turn the PJ top Right side out, and press.

Figure 1

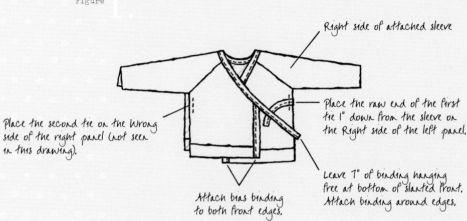

Right side of attached sleeve

Place the raw end of the first tie 1" down from the sleeve on the Right side of the left panel.

Place the second tie on the Wrong side of the right panel (not seen in this drawing).

Leave 7" of binding hanging free at bottom of slanted front. Attach binding around edges.

Attach bias binding to both front edges.

Figure 2

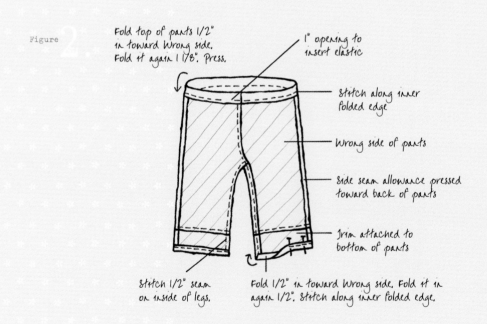

Fold top of pants 1/2" in toward Wrong side. Fold it again 1 1/8". Press.

1" opening to insert elastic

Stitch along inner folded edge

Wrong side of pants

Side seam allowance pressed toward back of pants

Trim attached to bottom of pants

Stitch 1/2" seam on inside of legs.

Fold 1/2" in toward Wrong side. Fold it in again 1/2". Stitch along inner folded edge.

pj pants or shorts

FOLLOW INSTRUCTIONS BELOW TO MAKE EITHER THE PANTS OR SHORTS.

• STEP 1 •

Attach the trim to the PJ pants.

a. Place the first front trim's top edge and the front pant's bottom edge Right sides together. Pin in place. Sew them together with a ½" seam, backstitching at each end. Zigzag or serge the seam allowance, then press it toward the bottom.

b. Repeat to attach the second front trim to other front pant.

c. Repeat to attach both the back trims to the bottom of each back pant.

• STEP 2 •

Attach the front and back of the PJ pants.

a. Place the two front pants Right sides together, matching the edges. Pin them together along the crotch. Stitch a ½" seam along the pinned edge, backstitching at each end. Zigzag or serge the seam allowance, then press it to one side.

b. Repeat to attach the two back pants together.

c. Open up the front and back pants. Place them Right sides together, matching the side edges, and pin them in place. Stitch a ½" seam down both outside edges, backstitching at each end. Zigzag or serge the seam allowance, then press it toward the back. (FIGURE 2)

d. Pin the legs' inseam together. Stitch a ½" seam along the matched edges, backstitching at each end. Zigzag or serge the seam allowance, then press it toward the back.

• STEP 3 •

Make the casing, and insert elastic around the waist.

a. Fold the pants' top edge in ½" toward the Wrong side, and press it flat.

b. Fold the same edge in again, this time by 1 ⅛", and press it. Pin the edge in place. Edge stitch around the inner folded edge, leaving a 1" opening next to the back seam. (FIGURE 2)

c. Attach the safety pin to one end of the elastic. Insert the pin through the opening. Thread the elastic through the casing, then back out the same opening. Be careful not to twist the elastic. Sew the ends together with a ½" seam, backstitching at each end. Push the joined ends of the elastic into the opening, and edge stitch the opening closed. Backstitch at each end.

• STEP 4 •

Hem pants. (FIGURE 2)

a. Fold one pant leg's bottom edge ½", toward the Wrong side, and press. Fold it in again ½", and press. Pin in place. Edge stitch along the inner folded edge, backstitching at each end.

b. Repeat to hem the other pant leg.

c. Turn the pants Right side out, and press.

chapter: 3.0 baby style

* COMFY JUMPER DRESS WITH BLOOMERS * TWO VERY CUTE HATS * CUTIE BOOTIES * EASY EMPIRE-WAIST TOP

every baby deserves
a little fashion. No need to sacrifice
comfort for great baby style. Like
I say, "Utility can be beautiful."
A comfy jumper, adorable hats,
modern booties, and an Asian-
inspired empire-waist top will
let the world know this baby
has arrived.

COMFY JUMPER DRESS WITH BLOOMERS ⇒

instructions: <u>P.60</u>

DIFFICULTY LEVEL 3

DIFFICULTY LEVEL *3*

f.

TWO VERY CUTE HATS ⇒

instructions: *P.65*

CUTIE BOOTIES ⇒

instructions: _P.72_

DIFFICULTY LEVEL 3

EASY EMPIRE-WAIST TOP ⇒

instructions: *P.75*

DIFFICULTY LEVEL 4

comfy jumper dress WITH BLOOMERS

finished size: 0–3 months, 3–6 months, 6–9 months, 9–12 months
difficulty level: 3

What will this year's baby be wearing? Here's an adorable getup that can be customized with your fabric choices. Elastic-waist bloomers (see page 63) keep diapers in place under a sleeveless jumper with pleats and button closures at shoulders.

FABRICS

For Jumper sizes 0–3 and 3–6 months

* ⅜ yard (44" wide) mid-weight print for the bodice, bodice lining, and band

* ⅜ yard (44" wide) second mid-weight print for the skirt

* ⅜ yard (44" wide) muslin for the skirt lining

For Jumper sizes 6–9 and 9–12 months

* ½ yard (44" wide) mid-weight print for the bodice, bodice lining, and band

* ½ yard (44" wide) second mid-weight print for the skirt

* ½ yard (44" wide) muslin for the skirt lining

For Bloomers

* ⅜ yard (44" wide) mid-weight print (for all sizes)

OTHER SUPPLIES

For Jumper

* Wax-free tracing paper by Prym-Dritz

* Tracing wheel

* Medium-size safety pin

* 1 spool coordinating all-purpose thread (we use Coats Dual Duty Plus)

* Two ⅜"-wide 2-hole flat buttons

* ¼ yard (¼" wide) elastic

For Bloomers

* 1 spool coordinating all-purpose thread (we use Coats Dual Duty Plus)

* Medium-size safety pin

* ¾ yard (1" wide) elastic for the waist

* ⅝ yard (¼" wide) elastic for the legs

jumper

• STEP 1 •

Cut out the pattern pieces.

From the pattern sheet included with this book, cut out:

- Bodice front
- Bodice back
- Skirt front
- Skirt back

• STEP 2 •

Cut out all of the pieces from the fabric.

a. Fold the fabrics in half, Wrong sides together, matching the selvage edges*. Gently press a crease in the fold. Open up the fabric. Then fold the selvage edges in to meet the center crease.

b. From the first print, cut:

- 2 bodice fronts on the fold (see General Notes, page 13)
- 2 bodice backs on the fold

Unfold the first fabric. Measure and mark the dimensions for the bands directly onto the Right side of the fabric. Cut along the marked lines.

- 1 front band
  - 0–3 months: 2" wide x 9" long
  - 3–6 months: 2" wide x 10" long
  - 6–9 months: 2" wide x 11" long
  - 9–12 months: 2" wide x 12" long

- 1 back band
  - 0–3 months: 2" wide x 10" long
  - 3–6 months: 2" wide x 11" long
  - 6–9 months: 2" wide x 12" long
  - 9–12 months: 2" wide x 13" long

c. From the second print, cut:

- 1 skirt front on the fold
- 1 skirt back on the fold

Unfold the second fabric, and cut:

- 1 loop: 1" wide x 2 ⅛" long

d. From the muslin for the lining, cut:

- 1 skirt front on the fold
- 1 skirt back on the fold

e. From the ¼"-wide elastic for the back of the jumper, cut:

- 1 piece
  - 0–3 months: 2 ½" long
  - 3–6 months: 3" long
  - 6–9 months: 4" long
  - 9–12 months: 5" long

• STEP 3 •

Transfer the lines* and marks* from the pattern piece to the fabric.

a. Use tracing paper*, a tracing wheel* or a chalk pencil, and the pattern piece as a guide. Transfer the marks and lines for the size you are making.

b. Transfer the marks for the pleats onto the Right side of the front and back skirts.

c. Repeat to transfer the marks for the pleats onto the Right side of each skirt lining.

d. Transfer the lines for the buttonholes onto the Right side of the exterior front bodice.

e. Transfer the stitching line and dot for the front slit onto the Wrong side of the front bodice.

f. Transfer the marks for attaching the buttons onto the Right side of the exterior back bodice.

Figure

Right side of front bodice

Edge stitch across folded edge on band.

match raw edges of band with bottom raw edge of front bodice.

machine baste just short of 1/2" across matched edges.

Attach the band to the exterior bodice pieces.

a. Fold the front band in half lengthwise, Wrong sides together, and press. Match the band's long edges with the front bodice's bottom edge, and pin it in place. Machine baste* just short of the ½" seam across the matched edges. Edge stitch* across the folded edge on the band, and backstitch* at each end. (FIGURE 1)

b. Repeat to attach the band to the exterior back bodice piece.

c. Place the exterior front and back bodice pieces Right sides together, matching the side edges. Pin them in place. Stitch a ½" seam down the sides, backstitching at each end. Press the seam allowances* open.

d. Repeat step 4c to attach the lining front and back bodice pieces together at the sides.

• STEP 5 •

Make the bodice.

a. Place the exterior and the lining bodice pieces Right sides together, matching the side seams and all the edges. Pin them in place.

b. Stitch a ½" seam all the way across the top of the back bodice, over the shoulder straps, around the armholes, and across the front to the center crease. Follow the stitching line at the center crease to make the front slit, pivoting* on the dot at the center point. Continue stitching along the top edge, stopping at the stitching where you began sewing. Backstitch at each end.

c. Trim* the seam allowances to ¼". Clip* the corners and curves in the seam allowance, being careful not to clip your stitching.

d. Turn the bodice Right side out, using a turning tool* to push out the corners. Press the bodice flat.

e. Match the bottom edges of the exterior and bodice lining, and pin them together. Machine baste a ½" seam around the bottom of the bodice, then trim the edges even.

• STEP 6 •

Make the buttonholes, and attach the buttons.

a. Make a buttonhole* on each strap at the marked lines on the front bodice's top rounded straps.

b. Hand-stitch one button at each mark on the Right side of the bodice back's top straps.

• STEP 7 •

Make pleats on the skirt and the skirt lining, and assemble the skirt.

a. Fold the skirt front, Right sides together, matching the marks for the first pleat. Pin the marks together. Stitch a 1" seam, ¾" in length, down the folded edge, and backstitch at each end. On the Wrong side of the skirt front, center the pleat over the seam, and machine baste across the top edges.

b. Repeat to make the other pleat on the skirt front and both pleats on the skirt back.

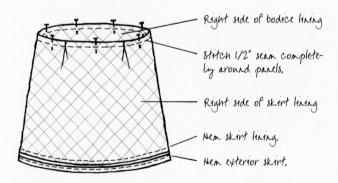

Figure

Right side of bodice lining

Stitch 1/2" seam completely around panels.

Right side of skirt lining

Hem skirt lining.

Hem exterior skirt.

c. Place the skirt front and back Right sides together, matching the side edges. Pin them in place. Stitch a ½" seam down the side edges, backstitching at each end. Zigzag or serge the seam allowance down the side edges, then trim any excess fabric.

d. Repeat steps 7a through 7c to make two pleats on both the front and back skirt lining pieces, and attach the front and back together.

Hem the skirt. (FIGURE 2)

a. Fold the bottom edge of the skirt exterior ½" in, toward the Wrong side, and press. Fold in again ½", and press. Pin along the inner folded edge, and then edge stitch along this edge, backstitching at each end.

b. Fold the bottom edge of the skirt lining ½" in, toward the Wrong side, and press. Fold in again 1", and press. Pin along the inner folded edge, and then edge stitch along this edge, backstitching at each end.

Attach the skirt to the bodice. (FIGURE 2)

a. Place the exterior and the lining of the skirt Wrong sides together, matching the top edges and pleats. Pin them in place. Machine baste a ½" seam around the top of the skirt.

b. Place the exterior skirt and the bodice Right sides together. Match the side seams and pin them in place. Stitch a ½" seam completely around the panels, backstitching at each end. Zigzag or serge the seam allowance, then trim any excess fabric.

c. On the back bodice seam allowance, measure and mark 2" in from each side seam. Place the end of the elastic piece at the first mark, and pin it in place. Stretch the other end of the elastic to the other mark, and pin it in place. Use a large zigzag stitch to sew across the elastic in the seam allowance while pulling it flat, and backstitch at each end.

- -

bloomers

Cut out the pattern piece.

From the pattern sheet included with this book, cut out:

- Front pant / Back pant

Cut out all of the pieces from the fabric.

a. Fold the fabric in half, Wrong sides together, matching the selvage edges*.

b. Follow the cutting line for your desired size. Use the entire pattern piece for the back pant. Fold the pattern piece back at the cutting line for the front pant.

c. From the print, cut:
- 2 front pants
- 2 back pants

d. From the 1" elastic for waist, cut:
- 1 waistband
  - 0–3 months: 19" long
  - 3–6 months: 20" long
  - 6–9 months: 21" long
  - 9–12 months: 22" long

e. From the ¼" elastic, cut:
- 2 leg bands
  - 0–3 months: each 8 ½" long
  - 3–6 months: each 9" long
  - 6–9 months: each 9 ½" long
  - 9–12 months: each 10" long

Sew the fabric pieces together.

a. Place the two front pants Right sides together, matching the edges. Pin the pieces together down the front crotch. Stitch a ½" seam along the pinned edge, backstitching* at each end. Zigzag or serge the seam allowance*, and press it to one side.

b. Repeat to attach the two back pants together.

c. Unfold the front and back pants. Place them Right sides together matching the side edges, and pin them in place. Stitch a ½" seam down both sides, backstitching at each end. Zigzag or serge the seam allowances. Press them toward the back pants.

d. Pin the inside leg edges together. Stitch a ½" seam on the inside of the legs, backstitching at each end. Zigzag or serge the seam allowance, and press toward the back pants.

• STEP 4 •

Make the casing, and insert the elastic around the waist. (FIGURE 3)

a. Fold the top edge of the pants ½" toward the Wrong side, and press.

b. Fold the edge in again, this time 1 ⅛", and press. Pin along the inner folded edge. Edge stitch* around the inner folded edge, leaving a 1" opening next to the back seam.

c. Attach the safety pin to one end of the elastic. Insert the pin through the opening. Thread the elastic through the casing, then back out the same opening. Be careful not to twist the elastic. Sew the ends together with a ½" seam, backstitching at each end. Push the joined ends of the elastic into the opening. Edge stitch the opening closed, backstitching at each end.

• STEP 5 •

Hem the bloomers. (FIGURE 3)

a. Starting on the first pant leg, fold the bottom edge ¼" toward the Wrong side, and press. Fold it in again 1 ½", and press. Pin the folded edge in place. Edge stitch along the inner folded edge, leaving 1" open on the inside of the leg, and backstitch at each end. Stitch another line ⅜" from the first stitching line, creating a casing for the elastic. Do not leave an opening.

b. Attach the safety pin to one end of the elastic, and insert it through the opening. Thread the elastic through the casing and out the same opening. Make sure not to twist the elastic.

c. Attach both ends of the elastic together with a ½" seam, backstitching at each end. Push the joined ends of the elastic into the opening. Edge stitch the opening closed, backstitching at each end.

d. Repeat to hem the other pant leg.

e. Turn the bloomers Right side out, and press.

Figure

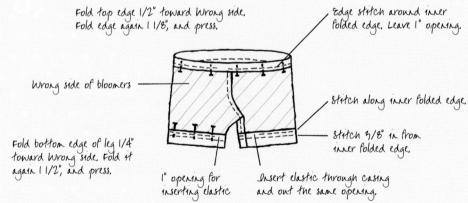

Fold top edge 1/2" toward Wrong side. Fold edge again 1 1/8", and press.

Edge stitch around inner folded edge. Leave 1" opening.

Wrong side of bloomers

stitch along inner folded edge.

stitch 3/8" in from inner folded edge.

Fold bottom edge of leg 1/4" toward Wrong side. Fold it again 1 1/2", and press.

1" opening for inserting elastic

Insert elastic through casing and out the same opening.

two very cute hats

finished hat size: 0–3 months: 14"; 3–6 months: 16"; 6–9 months: 18"; 9–12 months: 20"
difficulty level: 3

For hip baby boys and girls alike! A simple cap with a removable butterfly lets baby keep a fun toy close at hand. A miniature version of the military cap with a soft bill is a cinch to make and a charming way to get attention.

FABRICS

For Cap with Butterfly

* ¼ yard (44" or 54" wide) mid-weight fabric for the exterior

* ¼ yard (44" or 54" wide) mid-weight fabric for the lining

* 2 scraps coordinating fabric for the butterfly

For Military-Style Cap

* ½ yard (44" or 54" wide) mid-weight fabric for the exterior

* ⅜ yard (44" or 54" wide) mid-weight fabric for the lining

OTHER SUPPLIES

For Cap with Butterfly

* Medium-size safety pin

* ⅝ yard (¼" wide) elastic

* 4" (¾" wide) sew-on Velcro

* Wax-free tracing paper by Prym-Dritz

* Tracing wheel

* 1 spool coordinating all-purpose thread (we use Coats Dual Duty Plus)

* Tailor's ham* (optional)

* Sharp hand-sewing needle

* Handful of Nature-fil (all-natural premium fiberfill by Fairfield)

For Military-Style Cap

* ⅜ yard fusible fleece (we use Fusible Thermolam Plus by Pellon)

* ⅜ yard fusible woven interfacing (we use SF101 by Pellon)

* 1 spool coordinating all-purpose thread (we use Coats Dual Duty Plus)

* Sharp hand-sewing needle

cap with butterfly

· STEP 1 ·

Cut out the pattern piece.

From the pattern sheet included with this book, cut out:

- Crown

· STEP 2 ·

Cut out all of the pieces from the fabric.

a. Fold the fabric in half, Wrong sides together, matching the selvage edges*. Place the crown pattern piece on the bias* of the fabric, matching the grain line on the pattern piece with the lengthwise grain* of the fabric. Pin it in place.

b. From the exterior fabric, cut:
- 6 crowns on the bias

c. From the lining fabric, cut:
- 6 crowns on the bias

d. From the elastic, cut:
- 1 piece
  - 0–3 months: 14" long
  - 3–6 months: 16" long
  - 6–9 months: 18" long
  - 9–12 months: 20" long

e. From the Velcro, cut:
- 1 piece, 2" long
- 2 pieces, each 1" long

· STEP 3 ·

Transfer lines* for Velcro placement, and attach Velcro to the exterior of crown.

a. Use tracing paper*, a tracing wheel* or chalk pencil, and the pattern piece as a guide. Transfer the lines for Velcro placement from the pattern piece onto one exterior crown.

b. Round off all of the corners on both the male and female Velcro pieces.

c. Set the male half of the Velcro aside. (It will be used to attach to the butterfly's back.)

d. Place the female half of the Velcro within the marked placement lines, and pin them in place. Sew a large zigzag stitch completely around each piece, backstitching* at each end.

· STEP 4 ·

Sew the exterior pieces together. (FIGURE 1)

a. Place two exterior crown pieces Right sides together, matching the side edges, and pin down one side. Stitch a ½" seam down the matched edges, backstitching at each end. Press the seam allowances* open. Use a tailor's ham or a folded towel to press around the top curve.

b. Repeat the above step to attach the third crown piece to one unstitched side edge, making the first 3-panel section. Set it aside.

c. Repeat steps 4a and 4b to make the second 3-panel section of exterior crown pieces.

d. Place the two 3-panel sections Right sides together, matching the crown pieces at the tops of the sections. Pin them in place. Stitch a ½" seam across the matched edges, backstitching at each end. Press the seam allowance open.

· STEP 5 ·

Sew the lining pieces together.

Repeat step 4 to make the lining.

· STEP 6 ·

Sew the exterior and the lining together. (FIGURE 2)

a. Place the exterior and the lining Right sides together, matching the seams, and pin around the bottom raw edge. Stitch a ½" seam around the bottom edge, leaving a 3" opening along the edge and backstitching at each end.

b. Turn the cap Right side out, and push the lining inside the cap. Fold the unfinished edges of the opening under ½" and pin them closed. Press.

c. Topstitch* a ½" seam completely around the finished edge of the cap to create a casing for the elastic, and backstitch at each end. Remove the pins from the opening.

• STEP 7 •

Insert the elastic.

a. Attach the safety pin to one end of the elastic. Insert the pin into the opening. Thread the elastic through the casing and out the same opening. Be careful not to twist the elastic.

b. Attach both ends of the elastic together with a ½" seam, backstitching at each end. Push the joined ends of the elastic into the opening and pin it closed. Slipstitch* the opening closed.

Figure

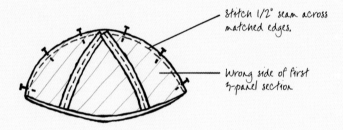

Stitch 1/2" seam across matched edges.

Wrong side of first 3-panel section

Figure

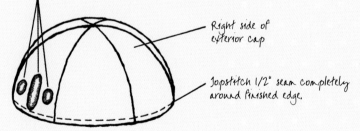

Female Velcro stitched on exterior crown

Right side of exterior cap

Topstitch 1/2" seam completely around finished edge.

butterfly

 note: Use a ¼" seam to make the butterfly.

• STEP 1 •

Cut out the pattern pieces.

From the pattern sheet included with this book, cut out:
- Upper wing
- Lower wing
- Body

• STEP 2 •

Cut out all of the pieces from the fabric.

a. Fold the fabric in half lengthwise, Wrong sides together. Use the pattern pieces to cut out the fabric pieces.

b. From the first fabric scrap, cut:
- 4 upper wings
- 4 lower wings

c. From the second fabric scrap, cut:
- 2 bodies

• STEP 3 •

Sew the upper and lower wings together.

a. Place the first upper and lower wings Right sides together, matching the center edges. Pin them in place. Stitch a ¼" seam across the matched edges, backstitching at each end. Press the seam allowance toward the bottom.

b. Repeat to attach the other three upper and lower wings.

• STEP 4 •

Attach the wings to the body.

a. Fold the butterfly body in half, matching the short, rounded edges. Gently press a crease to mark the center of the body.

b. Place the first wing and the body Right sides together, matching the center crease on the body with the center seam on the wing. Pin it in place. Stitch a ¼" seam to attach the wing, backstitching at each end. Press the seam allowance toward the wing.

c. Place the second wing onto the other side of the body, Right sides together. Pin it in place. Stitch a ¼" seam, ½" in length, at the top and bottom of the wing. The opening will be used to turn the butterfly Right side out and stuff.

d. Repeat to attach the other set of wings to the second body, except this time stitch all the way down the second wing— do not leave an opening.

• STEP 5 •

Attach Velcro to the butterfly back.

a. Center the butterfly back (the piece with the opening) on the cap's Velcro. Mark the placement for the male half of the Velcro on each wing. Center the 2" piece of male Velcro onto the body. Pin it in place. Then place the 1" pieces of male Velcro on each wing at the marks you just made. Pin them in place.

b. Use a large zigzag stitch and sew completely around each Velcro piece, backstitching at each end.

• STEP 6 •

Attach the front of the butterfly to the back. (FIGURE 3)

a. Place the front and back of the butterfly Right sides together, matching the outside edges. Stitch a ¼" seam completely around the outside edges, pivoting* at each corner and back-stitching at each end.

b. Clip* into the seam allowance around the wings, head, and tail. Make sure not to clip your stitching.

• STEP 7 •

Stuff the butterfly.

a. Turn the butterfly Right side out through the opening you left in Step 4. Push out the wings, head, and tail using a turning tool*. Press the butterfly flat.

b. Lightly fill the butterfly with fiberfill. Do not overstuff. Pin the opening closed.

c. With a hand-sewing needle and thread, slipstitch the opening closed.

d. Match the front and back seams on each side of the body, and pin them together. Stitch-in-the-ditch* between the wings and the body on each side, backstitching at each end.

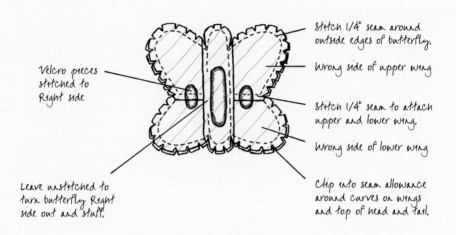

Velcro pieces
stitched to
Right side

Stitch 1/4" seam around
outside edges of butterfly.

Wrong side of upper wing

Stitch 1/4" seam to attach
upper and lower wing.

Wrong side of lower wing

Leave unstitched to
turn butterfly Right
side out and stuff.

Clip into seam allowance
around curves on wings
and top of head and tail.

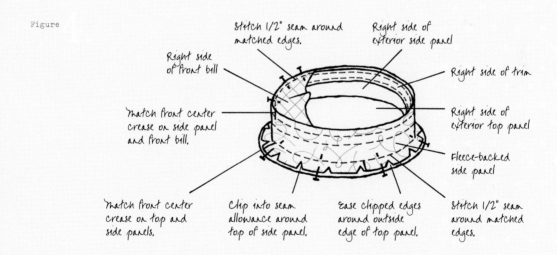

Stitch 1/2" seam around
matched edges.

Right side of
exterior side panel

Right side
of front bill

Right side of trim

Match front center
crease on side panel
and front bill.

Right side of
exterior top panel

Fleece-backed
side panel

Match front center
crease on top and
side panels.

Clip into seam
allowance around
top of side panel.

Ease chipped edges
around outside
edge of top panel.

Stitch 1/2" seam
around matched
edges.

military-style cap

• STEP 1 •

Cut out the pattern pieces.

From the pattern sheet included with this book, cut out:

- Top panel
- Front bill

• STEP 2 •

Cut out all of the pieces from the fabric.

a. Unfold the fabric. Fold over each selvage edge* 6" toward the Wrong side. Gently press a crease along the folded edges. Use the pattern pieces and the dimensions below to measure and mark directly onto Right side of fabric. Cut along the marked lines.

b. From the exterior fabric, cut:

- 1 top panel on the fold (see General Notes, page 13)
- 2 front bills on the fold

Unfold the exterior fabric, and cut:

- 1 side panel
  - 0–3 months: 15" wide x 2 ¾" long
  - 3–6 months: 17" wide x 3" long
  - 6–9 months: 19" wide x 3 ¼" long
  - 9–12 months: 21 ½" wide x 3 ½" long
- 1 trim
  - 0–3 months: 15" wide x 2 ¼" long
  - 3–6 months: 17" wide x 2 ½" long
  - 6–9 months: 19" wide x 2 ¾" long
  - 9–12 months: 21 ½" wide x 3" long

c. From the lining fabric, cut:

- 1 top panel on the fold

Unfold the lining fabric, and cut:

- 1 side panel
  - 0–3 months: 15" wide x 2 ¾" long
  - 3–6 months: 17" wide x 3" long
  - 6–9 months: 19" wide x 3 ¼" long
  - 9–12 months: 21 ½" wide x 3 ½" long

d. From the fusible fleece, cut:

- 1 top panel on the fold
- 1 bill on the fold

Unfold the fleece, and cut:

- 1 side panel
  - 0–3 months: 15" wide x 2 ¾" long
  - 3–6 months: 17" wide x 3" long
  - 6–9 months: 19" wide x 3 ¼" long
  - 9–12 months: 21 ½" wide x 3 ½" long

e. From fusible interfacing, cut:

- 1 top panel on the fold
- 1 front bill on the fold

Unfold the interfacing, and cut:

- 1 side panel
  - 0–3 months: 15" wide x 2 ¾" long
  - 3–6 months: 17" wide x 3" long
  - 6–9 months: 19" wide x 3 ¼" long
  - 9–12 months: 21 ½" wide x 3 ½" long

• STEP 3 •

Attach the interfacings.

a. Place the Wrong side of the exterior top and side panels, and one bill, on the top of the interfacing's fusible side. Use a pressing cloth*, and follow manufacturer's instruction to fuse them together.

b. Place the interfaced side of the exterior top and side panels, and the Wrong side of the second front bill, on top of the fleece's fusible side. Use a pressing cloth, and follow manufacturer's instruction to fuse them together.

• STEP 4 •

Make the front bill.

a. Place both bills Right sides together matching the outside curved edges, and pin them in place. Stitch a ½" seam around the outside curve, backstitching* at each end. Trim* the seam allowance* to ¼". Clip* into the seam allowance* every ½" to 1" around the curve.

b. Turn the bill Right side out, pushing out the curved edge. Match the inside raw edges, and pin them together. Press the bill flat.

c. Machine baste* a ½" seam around the unfinished edge. Clip into the curve's seam allowance.

• STEP 5 •

Attach the trim to the side panel.

a. Fold the trim in half lengthwise, Wrong sides together and press along the folded edge. Place the trim on the Right side of the side panel at the bottom edge, and pin it in place. Machine baste a seam across the matched edges, just short of ½" from the edge. Trim the bottom edges even.

b. Edge stitch* along the trim's top folded edge, backstitching at each end.

• STEP 6 •

Attach the side panel to the top panel.

a. Fold the side panel in half, Right sides together, matching the short edges. Press a center crease. Fold it in half again, and press.

b. Open the side panel one time so the short ends remain matched. Pin the short edges together. Stitch a ½" seam across the short edges, backstitching at each end. Press the seam allowance open. Topstitch* ½" on each side of center back seam, backstitching at each end.

c. Sew a ½" stay stitching* line around the top edge of side panel. Clip into the seam allowance every ½" to ¾".

d. Fold the top panel in half lengthwise, and then again across its width. Gently press the folded edges along the sides as a guide to attach the side panel.

e. Place the top and side panels Right sides together. Match the seam on side panel with the back crease on the top panel, then match the three other creases on each panel together. Ease the side panel around the edges of the top panel, and pin it in place. Stitch a ½" seam around matched edges, backstitching at each end. Press the seam allowance toward the side panel. (FIGURE 4, PAGE 69)

f. Topstitch a ¼" seam completely around the top of the side panel, backstitching at each end.

• STEP 7 •

Attach the front bill to the side panel.

a. Fold the bill in half lengthwise. Press a center crease along the raw edges on the inside curve. Place the bill and side panel Right sides together, matching the front center creases. Pin in place.

b. Stitch a ½" seam around the bill's inside curved edge, backstitching at each end. Press.

• STEP 8 •

Make and attach the lining to the hat's exterior.

a. Repeat Step 6 to make the lining for the hat.

b. With the hat's exterior Right side out and the lining Wrong side out, slip the lining over the exterior, matching the back seam and side and the front creases. Pin around the bottom edges. Stitch a ½" seam around the bottom edges, leaving a 4" opening along the side of the hat, and backstitch at each end.

c. Turn the hat Right side out through the 4" opening. Push the lining inside the hat, and press. Fold under ½" on each edge of the opening, and pin it closed. Slipstitch* the opening closed. Press along the finished seam.

d. Smooth the lining side panel up into hat. Pin though the exterior and the lining on the exterior of the hat. Stitch-in-the-ditch* along the top of the trim on the side panel. Sew completely around the bottom edge of the trim, backstitching at each end.

CUTIE BOOTIES

finished size: 0–3 months, 3–6 months, 6–9 months, 9–12 months
difficulty level: 3

These incredibly soft booties wrap and close with Velcro. No more maneuvering little feet into holes; these handy dandies load from the front.

FABRICS

* ¼ yard (44" or 54" wide) mid-weight fabric for the exterior
* ¼ yard (44" or 54" wide) mid-weight fabric for the lining

OTHER SUPPLIES

* ¼ yard (44" wide) fusible fleece (we use Fusible Thermolam Plus by Pellon)
* ½ yard (20" wide) fusible woven interfacing (we use SF101 by Pellon)
* 2" (¾" wide) sew-on Velcro
* Wax-free tracing paper by Prym-Dritz
* Tracing wheel
* Pressing cloth
* 1 spool coordinating all-purpose thread (we use Coats Dual Duty Plus)
* Hand towel for pressing
* Sharp hand-sewing needle

• STEP 1 •

Cut out the pattern pieces.

a. From the pattern sheet included with this book, cut out:
- Upper Panel
- Sole

b. Cut the pattern pieces to desired size, or trace and save the original pattern pieces for future use.

• STEP 2 •

Cut out all of the pieces from the fabric.

a. Fold the fabric in half lengthwise with Wrong sides together, matching the selvage* edges. Use the pattern pieces to cut out the fabric pieces.

b. From the exterior fabric, cut:
- 2 upper panels
- 2 soles

c. From the lining fabric, cut:
- 2 upper panels
- 2 soles

d. From the fusible fleece, cut:
- 2 upper panels
- 4 soles

e. From the fusible interfacing, cut:
- 2 upper panels
- 2 soles

f. From the Velcro, cut:

- 2 pieces, each 1" long

Round off the corners on both the male and female Velcro pieces.

• STEP 3 •

Transfer the lines* and marks* from the pattern piece to the fabric panels.

Use tracing paper*, a tracing wheel* or chalk pencil, and the pattern piece as a guide. Transfer the lines or marks for the size of booties you are making.

For the upper panel:

- Transfer the line for the female Velcro placement onto the Right side of the first exterior upper panel.
- Transfer the line for the female Velcro placement onto the second exterior upper panel by flipping the pattern piece so the writing side is facing the Right side of the fabric.
- Transfer the line for the male Velcro placement onto the Right side of the first lining upper panel.
- Transfer the line for the male Velcro placement onto the second lining upper panel by flipping the pattern piece so the writing side is facing the Right side of the fabric.
- Transfer notches* A and B onto the Right side of each exterior upper panel to mark where to overlap the front of the panel.
- Transfer the marks onto the Wrong side of each lining upper panel to mark the center of the front and the back of the bootie.

For the sole:

- Transfer notch C onto the Right side of the first exterior sole. Then transfer it to the second sole by flipping the pattern piece over so the writing side is facing the Right side of the other side.
- Transfer the marks for the center front and back onto the Wrong side of each of the exterior soles and onto the Right side of each of the lining soles.

• STEP 4 •

Attach the interfacings to the fabric pieces.

a. Place the Wrong side of both exterior upper panels and soles on top of the corresponding interfacing piece's fusible side. Use a pressing cloth*, and follow the manufacturer's instructions to fuse them together.

b. Place the Wrong side of both the exterior upper panels and the soles (with interfacing) on top of the fusible side of the corresponding fleece pieces. Use a pressing cloth, and follow manufacturer's instructions to fuse them together.

c. Trim ½" off completely around the other two fleece soles.

d. Center the fusible side of the trimmed fleece soles onto the Wrong side of each lining sole. Use a pressing cloth, and follow manufacturer's instructions to fuse each together.

• STEP 5 •

Attach Velcro to the upper panel.

a. On the Right side of the first exterior upper panel, center a 1" piece of female Velcro within the marked placement lines, and pin in place. Sew a large zigzag stitch around the Velcro, backstitching* at each end. Repeat to attach the other piece of female Velcro onto the second exterior upper panel.

b. On the Right side of the first lining upper panel, center a 1" piece of male Velcro within the marked placement lines, and pin it in place. Sew a large zigzag stitch around the Velcro, backstitching at each end. Repeat to attach the other piece of male Velcro onto the second lining upper panel.

• STEP 6 •

Make the upper panel.

a. Place the first exterior and lining upper panels Right sides together. Pin around the edges. Starting at the upper panel's bottom left corner, stitch a ½" seam up and around the front flap and across the center top, stopping at the top right corner and backstitching at each end. Trim the seam allowance* to ¼". Clip* into the seam allowance around the curves.

b. Turn the upper panel Right side out, pushing out the finished edges. Press the upper panel flat. Match the raw edges and pin them in place.

c. On the upper panel, place notch A on top of notch B and pin them in place. Attach the male to the female Velcro.

d. Sew a ½" stay stitching* line completely around the upper panel's bottom edge, backstitching at each end. Clip into the seam allowance every ½" to ¾" around the edges.

• STEP 7 •

Attach the upper panels to the soles.

a. Turn the lining side of the upper panel facing out.

b. Place the exterior upper panel onto the exterior sole with the Right sides together. Match the center-front and center-back marks on each, and pin them in place. Match notch A/B on the upper panel with notch C on the sole, and pin them in place. Ease the upper panel's edges around the sole's curves, pinning them in place. Stitch a ½" seam around the edges, backstitching at each end. (FIGURE 1)

c. Trim the seam allowance to ¼". Clip into the seam allowance around the front and back curves. Make sure not to clip the stitching.

d. Tightly roll up a hand towel and place one end inside the bootie. Press the seam allowance toward the sole using a pressing cloth.

• STEP 8 •

Attach the sole lining inside the bootie.

a. Fold ½" of the sole lining toward the fleece side, and press the edges. Pin and machine baste* the raw edge in place.

b. With the lining side of the bootie still facing out, place the fleece side of the lining and exterior soles together. Match the center-front and center-back marks, and pin them in place. Pin the sole in place around the remaining edges.

c. Slipstitch* around the sole's folded edges.

d. Remove the machine basting on the sole lining.

e. Turn the bootie Right side out, and press around the edges.

• STEP 9 •

Repeat steps 6 through 8 to make the bootie for opposite foot.

Figure

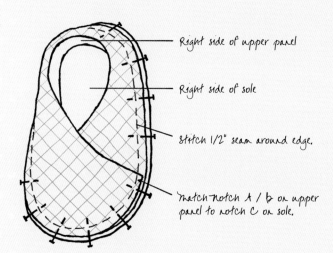

Right side of upper panel

Right side of sole

Stitch 1/2" seam around edge.

match notch A / b on upper panel to notch C on sole.

easy empire-waist top

finished size: 0–3 months, 3–6 months, 6–9 months, 9–12 months
difficulty level: 4

Your little emperor or empress will rule the family in this elegant Asian-style design. With a soft V-neck and tie, and a one-button closure in the back, it's easy to put on and take off and offers maximum comfort for baby. Pair with bloomers in a complementary fabric from the Comfy Jumper Dress (page 60) for a truly royal look.

FABRICS

For sizes 0–3 and 3–6 months

* ⅜ yard (44" wide) mid-weight print for the bodice and bodice lining
* ¾ yard (44" wide) second mid-weight print for the lower panel, sleeves, trim, and tie

For sizes 6–9 and 9–12 months

* ½ yard (44" wide) mid-weight print for the bodice and bodice lining
* ¾ yard (44" wide) second mid-weight print for the lower panel, sleeves, trim, and tie

OTHER SUPPLIES

* Wax-free tracing paper by Prym-Dritz
* Tracing wheel
* 1 spool coordinating all-purpose thread (we use Coats Dual Duty Plus)
* One ⅜"-wide shank-style button
* ⅜ yard (¼" wide) elastic

NOTE

* See page 63 for instructions on making bloomers.

• STEP 1 •

Cut out the pattern pieces.

From the pattern sheet included with this book, cut out:

- Front bodice
- Back bodice
- Front trim
- Back trim

• STEP 2 •

Cut out all of the pieces from the fabric.

a. Fold the fabric in half Wrong sides together, matching the selvage edges*. Use the pattern pieces, following the line for the size of top you are making.

b. From the first print, cut:

- 2 front bodices on the fold (see General Notes, page 13)
- 4 back bodices

c. From the second print, cut:

- 1 front trim on the fold
- 2 back trims

d. For the following pieces, measure and mark the dimensions for the size top you are making directly onto the Right side of the second print. Cut along the marked lines:

- 2 lower panels
    - 0–3 months: 14 ½" wide x 12 ¼" long
    - 3–6 months: 15" wide x 13" long
    - 6–9 months: 15 ½" wide x 13 ¾" long
    - 9–12 months: 16" wide x 14 ½" long

- 2 sleeves
    - 0–3 months: 10 ½" wide x 10 ¼" long
    - 3–6 months: 11 ½" wide x 10 ¾" long
    - 6–9 months: 12 ½" wide x 11 ¼" long
    - 9–12 months: 13 ½" wide x 11 ¾" long

Unfold the fabric, and cut:
- 1 tie: 1 ¼" wide x 16" long
- 1 loop: 1" wide x 2 ⅛" long

e. From the elastic for the front and back of the top, cut:
- 2 pieces
    - 0–3 months: each 2 ½" long
    - 3–6 months: each 3" long
    - 6–9 months: each 4" long
    - 9–12 months: each 5" long

• STEP 3 •

Transfer the lines* and marks* from the pattern piece to the fabric panels.

a. Use tracing paper*, a tracing wheel* or a chalk pencil, and the pattern piece as a guide. Transfer the lines and marks for the size top you are making.

b. Measure and mark on the Wrong side of the front lower panel, 3 ½" up from the bottom edge on each side edge for the slits.

c. Transfer the dot* onto the Right side of the center front trim.

d. Transfer the dot onto the Wrong side of the center front bodice.

e. Transfer the mark onto the Wrong side along the center back edge of the back bodice for the starting point for stitching the back.

• STEP 4 •

Make the bodice.

a. Place both exterior back bodice pieces Right sides together, and pin along the center back edges. Starting at the mark you just made, stitch a ½" seam to the bottom edges, and backstitch* at each end. Press the seam allowance* open.

b. Place the front and back bodice pieces Right sides together, matching the shoulder edges, and pin them in place. Stitch a ½" seam across each shoulder, backstitching at each end. Press the seam allowances open.

c. Repeat steps 4a and 4b to make the bodice lining. Set aside.

• STEP 5 •

Make and attach the trim to the bodice. (FIGURE 1)

a. Place the front and back trim pieces Right sides together, matching the shoulder edges, and pin them in place. Stitch a ½" seam across each shoulder, backstitching at each end. Press the seam allowances open.

b. Machine baste* a ½" seam along the outside edge of the trim.

c. Fold under ½" toward the Wrong side at the basting stitch, along the outside edge of the front and back trim. Press along the folded edge.

d. Place the Wrong side of the trim onto the Right side of the bodice, matching the raw edges around the inside of the neck, and pin in place. Machine baste a just-short-of ½" seam around the inside raw edges, pivoting* at the center dot on the front trim. Edge stitch* around the outside folded edge of the trim, backstitching at each end. Topstitch* ½" from the edge stitching for detail, and backstitch at each end.

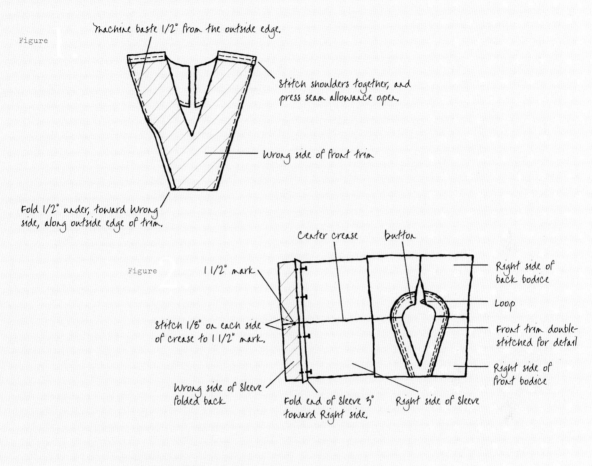

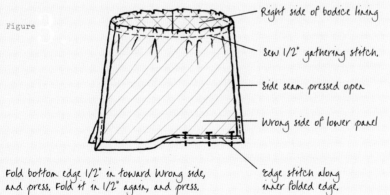

Figure

machine baste 1/2" from the outside edge.

Stitch shoulders together, and press seam allowance open.

Wrong side of front trim

Fold 1/2" under, toward wrong side, along outside edge of trim.

Figure

Center crease

button

1 1/2" mark

Right side of back bodice

Loop

Stitch 1/8" on each side of crease to 1 1/2" mark.

Front trim double-stitched for detail

Right side of front bodice

Wrong side of sleeve folded back

Fold end of sleeve ½" toward Right side.

Right side of sleeve

Figure

Right side of bodice lining

Sew 1/2" gathering stitch.

Side seam pressed open

Wrong side of lower panel

Fold bottom edge 1/2" in toward wrong side, and press. Fold it in 1/2" again, and press.

Edge stitch along inner folded edge.

Make and attach loop to the bodice.

a. To make the loop, follow instructions for making a strap (see page 172).

b. Fold the finished loop in half, matching the short ends. On the Right side of the back panel, place the ends of the loop side by side, even with the left center back edge, placing it ½" down from the top edge. Pin it in place. Machine baste a ½" seam across the ends of the loop.

Attach the lining to the bodice.

a. Place the exterior and lining bodices Right sides together, matching the inside edges around the neck opening and down the center back edges. Pin them in place. Starting at the mark you made in step 3e on the center back edge, stitch a ½" seam, stopping ½" from the top of the back bodice. Keeping your needle in the down position, turn the bodice and continue stitching around the inside edges of the neck opening to the dot at the center front bodice. Pivot at the dot and continue stitching up the other side, turning the bodice again ½" from the other back corner, and finishing at the mark on the other center back edge. Backstitch at each end.

b. Trim the corners in the seam allowance. Trim the seam allowances to ¼". Clip* into the seam allowance around the curved edges and to the dot at the center of the front bodice. Then clip to the mark in the seam allowance where you began stitching on the center back edges. Make sure not to clip the stitching. Repeat to clip the seam allowances at the mark on the back lining.

c. Turn the bodice Right side out, matching the center back and bottom edges. Use a turning tool* to push out the corners. Press the seams flat.

d. Pin and machine baste just short of ½" from the matched raw edges.

e. Match the top finished edges of the back bodices with the Right side facing up. Make a mark for the button placement opposite the loop.

f. Hand-stitch the button in place on the mark.

Attach the sleeves to the bodice, and hem.

a. Fold the first sleeve in half lengthwise, Right sides together. Gently press a center crease. Open up the sleeve.

b. Place the top edge of the first sleeve and left side edge of the bodice Right sides together, matching the shoulder seam and center crease. Pin in place. Stitch a ½" seam across the matched edges, backstitching at each end. Zigzag or serge the seam allowance. Trim the excess fabric in the seam allowance.

c. Fold the end of the sleeve ½" in toward the Wrong side, and press.

d. Fold the same end of the sleeve 3" back toward the Right side, and gently press along the folded edge. Pin it in place while you mark and stitch the slit. Measure and mark ⅛" on each side of the center crease at the folded edge. Then, starting at the folded edge, measure and mark 1 ½" up on the center crease. Starting at one of the ⅛" marks on one side of the center crease, sew to the 1 ½" mark on the center crease, pivot at the mark, and stitch to the other ⅛" mark, backstitching at each end. (FIGURE 2)

e. With scissors, cut along the center crease to the point of the stitching line, making sure not to cut the stitching.

f. Turn the sleeve's end Right side out. Use a turning tool to gently push out the corners of the slit. Press it flat.

g. Place the front and back bodices Right sides together, folding the sleeve in half lengthwise, and matching the raw edges. Pin it in place. Stitch a ½" seam down the sleeve, stopping at the seam that attaches it to the bodice. Pivot and continue stitching the ½" seam on the side of the bodice, backstitching at each end. Clip into the seam allowance at the seam that attaches the sleeve to the bodice, making sure not to clip the stitching. Zigzag or serge the seam allowance. Trim the excess fabric. Press the seam allowance toward the back.

h. Fold the end of the sleeve 3" toward the Wrong side, and pin along the inner folded edge. Edge stitch along the inner folded edge, backstitching at each end. Topstitch ½" from the edge stitching, backstitching at each end.

i. Repeat steps 8a through 8h to attach the sleeve, make the slit, and hem the other sleeve.

• STEP 9 •

Make the lower panel.

a. Place the front and back lower panels Right sides together. Pin down the side edges.

b. Stitch a ½" seam down both side edges, stopping at the marks 3 ½" from the bottom edge, and backstitching at each end. Press the seam allowances open.

• STEP 10 •

Hem the lower panel. (FIGURE 3)

a. Starting at the bottom of the first side seam, fold the edge on one side of the seam allowance ¼" in toward the Wrong side, and press. Fold it again ¼" in, and press. Pin in place. Repeat to fold under the other edge of the seam allowance and both edges on the other side.

b. Starting at the bottom of the side slit, edge stitch along the inner folded edge, turning at the top of the slit. Stitch across the seam allowance to the other side and turn again, stitching down the other side of the slit, and backstitching at each end. Repeat to finish the seam allowances for the other slit on the opposite side of the lower panel.

c. Fold the bottom of the first lower panel ½" in toward the Wrong side, and press. Fold in ½" again, and press. Pin in place. Edge stitch across the inner folded edge, backstitching at each end. Repeat to hem the other lower panel.

• STEP 11 •

Attach the lower panel to the bodice.

a. Find the center of both the front and back lower panels by folding them in half lengthwise, matching the side seams. Press a crease at the top 1" on the front and again at the back of the lower panel to mark the center of each side.

b. Sew a ½" gathering stitch* around the lower panel's top edge. Pull the bobbin thread to gather the lower panel's top until it measures the same size as the bottom of the bodice. Insert a straight pin next to gathering threads, and make a figure eight with the ends of the thread around the pin to secure it.

note: The front of the bodice is gathered slightly more than the back. You will add elastic to the front and back to gather them in even more.

c. Place the bottom edge of the bodice and the top edge of the lower panel Right sides together. Match the center creases on the lower panel to center front and back of the bodice, and pin them together. Match the side seams on the bodice and the lower panel, and pin them in place. Evenly distribute gathers in each section, and finish pinning around the edges. Stitch a ½" seam around matched edges, backstitching at each end. Zigzag or serge the seam allowance. Trim the excess fabric. (FIGURE 3)

d. Measure and mark 2 ½" in from each side seam in the seam allowance on both the front and back lower panels.

e. Find the center of each piece of elastic and mark with a straight pin. Starting on the front lower panel, place one end of the first piece of elastic at the 2 ½" mark. Pin it in place. Place the other end at the opposite 2 ½" mark on the front lower panel. Pin it in place. Match the center pin on the elastic with the center crease on the front lower panel. Pin in place. Sew a large zigzag stitch across the elastic while pulling it flat in the seam allowance, backstitching at each end. Repeat to attach the second piece of elastic across the seam allowance on the back lower panel.

• STEP 12 •

Make and attach the tie.

a. Follow the instructions on page 172 to make a tie.

b. Fold the tie in half and mark the center with a straight pin. Center the tie on the Right side at middle of the front bodice, under the point of the neck opening. Pin the tie in place. Stitch across the center of it, back and forth a few times, to secure it in place, then tie it in a bow.

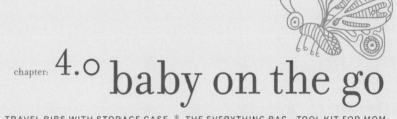

chapter: 4.0 baby on the go

* TRAVEL BIBS WITH STORAGE CASE * THE EVERYTHING BAG—TOOL KIT FOR MOM
* MODERN DIAPER BAG WITH CHANGING PAD

Who says diaper bags should be frumpy? Not me. In this chapter, you'll find practical yet fashionable tools for the road, including a modern diaper bag, an everything bag, and even a couple travel bibs—with their own storage case—for jet-setting tykes.

i.

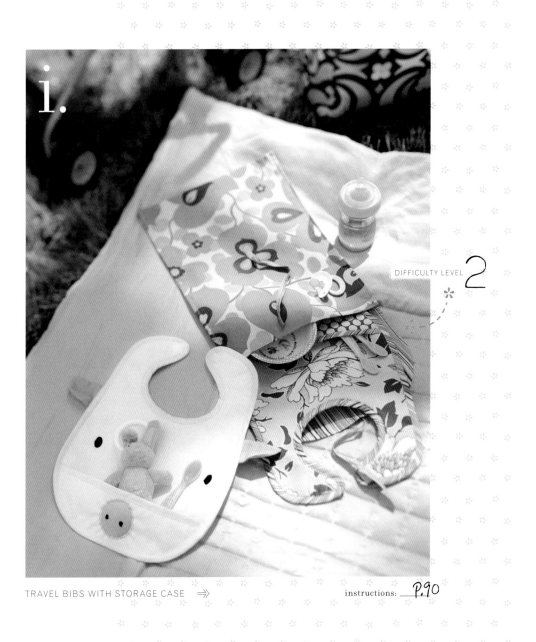

DIFFICULTY LEVEL 2

TRAVEL BIBS WITH STORAGE CASE ⟹   instructions: _P.90_

DIFFICULTY LEVEL 4

THE EVERYTHING BAG—TOOL KIT FOR MOM ⇒ instructions: _P.96_

k!

MODERN DIAPER BAG WITH CHANGING PAD ⟹

instructions: P.101

Travel BIBS WITH STORAGE CASE

piggy travel bib finished size: 10 ½" wide x 13 ¾" long
mixed-print travel bib finished size: 10 ½" wide x 13 ¾" long
storage case finished size: 11 ½" wide x 15" long
difficulty level: 2

Even bibs can be stylish (or downright humorous). Make them in little piggy or print fabric designs with simple Velcro closures and practical pockets. The handy carrying case holds a few bibs plus other small necessities.

FABRICS

For Piggy Travel Bib

* 1 yard (44" or 54" wide) mid-weight solid for the bib, binding, and front pouch

* 10" x 10" mid-weight fabric for the snout and ears

For Mixed-Print Travel Bib

* ½ yard (44" or 54" wide) mid-weight print for the front

* ½ yard (44" or 54" wide) coordinating mid-weight print for the back and the front pouch

* ½ yard (44" or 54" wide) additional coordinating mid-weight print for the single-fold bias binding

For Storage Case

* 1 yard (44" or 54" wide) mid-weight fabric for the exterior

* 1 yard (44" or 54" wide) coordinating mid-weight fabric for the lining and ties

OTHER SUPPLIES

For Piggy Travel Bib

* ½ yard (20" wide) mid-weight woven fusible interfacing (we use SF101 by Pellon)

* ½ yard (44" wide) fusible fleece (we use Fusible Thermolam Plus by Pellon)

* Wax-free tracing paper by Prym-Dritz

* Tracing wheel

* Tapestry needle (size 20 or 22)

* 1 skein coordinating perle cotton embroidery floss for face details

* 1 spool coordinating all-purpose thread (we use Coats Dual Duty Plus)

* Handful of Nature-fil (all-natural premium fiberfill by Fairfield)

* 1" (¾" wide) sew-on Velcro

For Mixed-Print Travel Bib

* ½ yard (20" wide) mid-weight woven fusible interfacing (we use SF101 by Pellon)

* ½ yard (44" wide) fusible fleece (we use Fusible Thermolam Plus by Pellon)

* 1 spool coordinating all-purpose thread (we use Coats Dual Duty Plus)

* 1" (¾" wide) Velcro

For Storage Case

* 1 ⅛ yards (20" wide) mid-weight woven fusible interfacing (we use SF101 by Pellon)

* Small dinner plate or cereal bowl (to mark curved edge on the flap of bag)

* 1 spool coordinating all-purpose thread (we use Coats Dual Duty Plus)

piggy travel bib

• STEP 1 •

Cut out the pattern pieces.

From the pattern sheet included with this book, cut out:

- Front/back panel
- Front pouch
- Piggy ear
- Piggy snout

• STEP 2 •

Cut out all of the pieces from the fabric.

a. Fold the fabric in half lengthwise, matching the selvage edges*, and press a center crease. Use pattern pieces to cut out the fabric pieces.

b. From the solid, cut:

- 1 front panel on the fold (see General Notes, page 13)
- 1 back panel on the fold
- 2 front pouch panels on the fold
- 60" of 1 ½" bias binding* strip

c. From the snout/ear fabric, cut:

- 1 snout
- 4 ears

note: Separate the ear pieces into two pairs. Each set will contain a front and back. Be sure that the point on each set is at the top of the ear.

d. From the fusible interfacing, cut:

- 1 front panel on the fold
- 1 front pouch on the fold
- 2 ears

e. From the fusible fleece, cut:

- 1 back panel on the fold

• STEP 3 •

Apply the fusible interfacing and fleece.

a. Place the front panel Right side up on the interfacing's fusible side. Follow the manufacturer's instructions to fuse, using an iron's "wool" setting.

b. Place the first front pouch Right side up on the interfacing's fusible side. Follow the manufacturer's instructions to fuse, using an iron's "wool" setting.

c. Place the first ear piece (front of Set 1) Right side up on the interfacing's fusible side. Follow the manufacturer's instructions to fuse, using an iron's "wool" setting.

d. Repeat to fuse interfacing to the second ear piece (front of Set 2).

e. Place the back panel Right side up on the fleece's fusible side. Follow the manufacturer's instructions to fuse, using an iron's "wool" setting.

• STEP 4 •

Embroider the eyes and nostrils, and attach the snout.

a. Using tracing paper* and a tracing wheel* or a chalk pencil, transfer the marks for the nostrils from the pattern piece onto the Right side of the snout. Transfer the marks for the eyes onto the Right side of the front panel and the marks for the ears onto the Right side of the back panel.

b. Embroider satin stitch* both eyes on the bib's front.

c. Embroider satin stitch the nostrils on the snout.

d. Find the center of the front pouch (with interfacing) by folding it in half across the width. Gently press a crease on the fold.

e. Find the center of the snout by folding it in half. Gently press a crease on the fold.

f. Pin the snout on the front pouch (with interfacing), matching the center creases. Center the snout from top to bottom on the front pouch. Pin it in place. Machine satin stitch, using a tight zigzag stitch, completely around the snout. Backstitch* at each end.

g. Cut a 1" slit in the front pouch panel only, behind the snout. Lightly stuff the snout with fiberfill. Whip stitch* the slit closed.

Make the front pouch.

a. Place the front pouch panel (with interfacing) and the second front pouch panel Wrong sides together, matching the raw edges. Machine baste* completely around all of the edges.

b. Apply single-fold bias binding* to the straight edge of the pouch. Use a ¼" seam (vs. ½").

• STEP 6 •

Attach the front pouch and the front and back panels.

a. Pin the front pouch to the front panel's bottom edge, matching the raw edges. Place the lining side of the front pouch onto the Right side of the front panel. Machine baste along the curved bottom edge.

b. Pin the front and back panels Wrong sides together. Machine baste around all the edges.

• STEP 7 •

Make the ears.

a. Place one ear panel with interfacing and one without interfacing Right sides together. Pin along the outer curved edges. Stitch a ½" seam along the pinned edges, using short stitches. Leave the straight edge unstitched. Trim the seam allowance* to ¼". Trim in the seam allowance straight across the point making sure not to clip your stitching. Turn the ear Right side out, using a turning tool* to push out the point of the ear. Press flat.

b. To make a pleat on the ear, fold the ear in half, Right sides together, across the width of the open end. Pin and then stitch a ¾" long seam, ⅜" from the folded edge. Unfold the ear. Press the pleat toward the ear's bottom. Machine baste across the ear's pleated edge. (FIGURE 1)

c. Repeat to make and pleat the second ear.

• STEP 8 •

Attach the ears and the binding. (FIGURE 2)

a. Pin the ears on each side of the bib's back, at the marks transferred from the pattern piece. Match the unfinished edge of the ear to the back's raw edge. Pin the ears with the back of the pleat facing the back panel. Machine baste ears in place.

b. Attach the single-fold bias binding. Use a ¼" seam.

c. After completing the single-fold bias binding, fold the ears to the front over the bias binding. Press, and pin in place. Sew the ears in place by stitching the length of the ear through the outer edge of the binding and ear.

• STEP 9 •

Complete the bib.

a. Pin the 1" female Velcro onto the lined side at the right top. Edge stitch* around the edges of the Velcro.

b. Pin the 1" male Velcro to the Right side at the left top. Edge stitch around the Velcro.

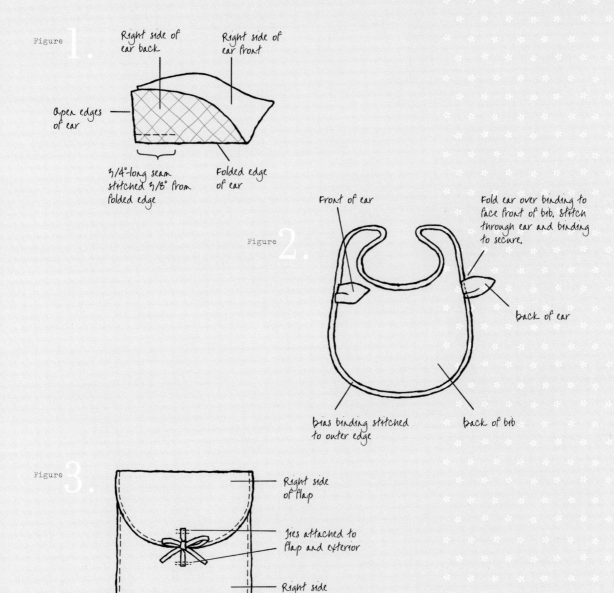

Figure 1.

Right side of ear back

Right side of ear front

Open edges of ear

3/4"-long seam stitched 3/8" from folded edge

Folded edge of ear

Figure 2.

Front of ear

Fold ear over binding to face front of bib. Stitch through ear and binding to secure.

back of ear

bias binding stitched to outer edge

back of bib

Figure 3.

Right side of flap

Ties attached to flap and exterior

Right side of exterior

Stitch 1/4" around all edges.

mixed-print travel bib

• STEP 1 •
Cut out the pattern pieces.

From the pattern sheet included with this book, cut out:
- Front/back panel
- Front pouch

• STEP 2 •
Cut out all of the pieces from the fabric.

a. From the first print, cut:
- 1 front panel on the fold

b. From the second print, cut:
- 1 back panel on the fold
- 2 front pouch panels on the fold

c. From the third print, cut:
- 60" of 1 ½" bias binding strip

d. From the fusible interfacing, cut:
- 1 front panel on the fold
- 1 front pouch on the fold

e. From the fusible fleece, cut:
- 1 back panel on the fold

• STEP 3 •
Make the Mixed-Print Travel Bib.

Follow instructions for the Piggy Travel Bib, omitting references to ears, snout, and eyes.

storage case

• STEP 1 •
Cut out all of the pieces from the fabric.

Measure and mark the dimensions directly onto the Right side of the fabric. Cut along the marked lines.

a. From the exterior fabric, cut:
- 1 exterior panel: 12 ½" wide x 31" long
- 1 flap panel: 12 ½" wide x 8" long

b. From the lining fabric, cut:
- 1 lining panel: 12 ½" wide x 31" long
- 1 flap panel: 12 ½" wide x 8" long
- 2 ties: each 1 ½" wide x 10" long

c. From the fusible interfacing, cut:
- 1 panel: 12 ½" wide x 31" long
- 1 flap panel: 12 ½" wide x 8" long

• STEP 2 •
Apply fusible interfacing.

a. Place the exterior panel Right side up on the interfacing's fusible side. Follow the manufacturer's instructions to fuse, using an iron's "wool" setting.

b. Place the exterior flap Right side up on the interfacing's fusible side. Follow the manufacturer's instructions to fuse, using an iron's "wool" setting.

• STEP 3 •
Make the ties.

Fold under each end of the first tie ¼" to the Wrong side and press. Repeat for the second tie. Follow the strap instructions on page 172 to complete the ties.

Make the flap.

a. Pin the exterior and lining flap panels Right sides together, matching the edges. Measure and mark 5" in and 3" up from each bottom corner.

b. Place the dinner plate upside down on top of the flaps. Match the edges of the plate to the side and bottom marks. Draw around the edge of the plate with fabric marker, connecting the marks on each edge. Cut all of the layers along the marked line. Pin the flap's curved edge. Stitch a ½" seam along the pinned, curved edge, backstitching at each end. Trim the seam allowance to ¼".

c. Turn the flap Right side out, and press. Machine baste across the open end.

d. Find the flap's center by folding it in half across the width. Gently press a crease on the fold. On the Right side of the flap, measure and mark 1 ¼" up from the finished edge on the center crease.

e. Pin one end of the first tie at the mark on the center crease, with the other end of the tie hanging below the finished edge of the flap. Stitch across the pinned end of the tie, backstitching at each end. Stitch ¼" below the first stitching line, backstitching at each end.

Attach the second tie to the exterior.

a. Find the center of the exterior by folding it in half, matching the long edges. Gently press a crease. On the Right side of the panel, measure 8 ½" down from the top edge on the center crease. Make a mark. Pin one end of the second tie at the mark, with the other end of the tie hanging past the top edge of the panel. Stitch across the pinned end of the tie, backstitching at each end. Stitch ¼" from the first stitching line, backstitching at each end.

b. Fold the exterior in half, Right sides together, matching the short ends. Pin down the side edges. Stitch a ½" seam down the matched edges, backstitching at each end.

Make the lining, and attach it to the exterior.

a. Fold the lining in half, Right sides together, matching the short ends. Pin the side edges. Stitch a ½" seam down the pinned edges, backstitching at each end.

b. Place the exterior side of the flap onto the Right side of the exterior panel without the tie attached. Match the raw edges and pin in place. Machine baste along the pinned edge.

c. With the exterior Right side out and the lining Wrong side out, slide the lining over the exterior, tucking the flap down between the panels. Match the side seams, and pin the top edges. Stitch a ½" seam around the pinned edge, leaving a 5" opening on the front, and backstitching at each end.

d. Turn the case Right side out and push the lining down inside the exterior, pulling out the flap. Press the top edge, then turn the raw edges under by ½". Pin in place.

e. Smooth the lining inside the exterior. Topstitch* ¼" from all the finished edges and around the flap, stitching through the exterior and lining. (FIGURE 3)

THE everyTHInG BaG—TOOL KIT FOR MOM

finished size: 16" wide x 11" tall (plus straps) x 6 ½" deep
difficulty level: 4

Emphasis on everything. Use this bag to carry baby supplies out and about or just from room to room. Multiple interior pockets make organizing easy, and a wide, flat bottom provides stability. Generously sized, it's screaming for your favorite fabric choices.

FABRICS

* 1 yard (44" or 54" wide) mid-weight print for the exterior

* 1 ¾ yards (44" or 54" wide) coordinating mid-weight print for the lining

OTHER SUPPLIES

* 1 yard (44" wide) fusible fleece (we use Fusible Thermolam Plus by Pellon)

* 2 ¾ yards (20" wide) mid-weight fusible woven interfacing (we use SF101 by Pellon)

* 1 yard (22" wide) single-sided fusible Peltex or a similar heavy-weight stabilizer

* 1 yard (¼" wide) elastic for pockets

* Medium-size safety pin

* 1 spool coordinating all-purpose thread (we use Coats Dual Duty Plus)

* Pressing cloth

• STEP 1 •

Cut out all of the pieces from the fabric.

a. Fold the fabric in half lengthwise, Wrong sides together, matching the selvage edges*. Gently press a center crease. Measure and mark the dimensions directly onto the Right side of the fabric. Cut along the marked lines.

b. From the first print, cut:

- 2 main panels, each 17" wide x 12" long
- 2 side panels, each 7 ½" wide x 12" long
- 4 side pockets, each 7 ½" wide x 7" long
- 1 bottom panel, 17" wide x 7 ½" long
- 2 straps, each 4" wide x 18" long

c. From the lining fabric, cut:

- 2 main panels, each 17" wide x 12" long
- 4 side panels, each 4 ¼" wide x 12" long
- 4 pocket panels, each 21" wide x 11" long
- 1 bottom panel, 17" wide x 7 ½" long
- 2 dividers, each 17" wide x 12" long

d. From the fusible fleece, cut:

- 2 main panels, each 17" wide x 12" long
- 2 side panels, each 7 ½" wide x 12" long
- 2 side pockets, each 7 ½" wide x 7" long
- 1 bottom panel, 17" wide x 7 ½" long

e. From the fusible interfacing, cut:

- 2 main panels, each 17" wide x 12" long
- 2 side panels, each 7 ½" wide x 12" long
- 2 side pockets, each 7 ½" wide x 7" long
- 1 bottom panel, 17" wide x 7 ½" long
- 2 pocket panels, each 21" wide x 11" long
- 2 straps, each 4" wide x 18" long

f. From fusible Peltex, cut:

- 2 bottom panels, each 6 ¼" wide x 15 ¾" long
- 2 dividers, each 16" wide x 11" long

g. From the elastic, cut:

- 2 pieces, each 15" long

· STEP 2 ·

Attach the interfacings.

a. Place the first exterior main panel Right side up on the interfacing's fusible side. Follow the manufacturer's instructions to fuse, using an iron's "wool" setting.

b. Place the same exterior main panel, with interfacing, Right side up on the fleece's fusible side. Follow the manufacturer's instructions to fuse, using an iron's "wool" setting.

c. Repeat the above step to fuse interfacing and fleece to the following panels:

- second exterior main panel
- both exterior side panels
- 2 side pockets

d. Repeat Step 2a to fuse interfacing to 2 pocket panels and both straps.

e. Place the exterior bottom panel Right side up on the interfacing's fusible side. Follow the manufacturer's instructions to fuse, using an iron's "wool" setting. Do not apply the fusible fleece at this point.

f. Center the Peltex panels on the Wrong side of the exterior bottom panel. Place the fleece's fusible side onto the Peltex. Follow the manufacturer's instructions to fuse, using an iron's "wool" setting.

g. Repeat Step 2f to fuse the 2 Peltex divider panels together. Place the fusible sides of the Peltex bottom panels together matching the outside edges. Fuse the Peltex in place.

· STEP 3 ·

Make the center divider. (FIGURE 1)

a. Place the first lining side panel and divider Right sides together. Pin the side edges. Stitch a ½" seam across the pinned edges, starting and stopping ½" in from the top and bottom edges, and backstitching* at each end.

b. Repeat the above step to attach the second lining side panel to the opposite end of the first divider.

c. Repeat to attach the last two lining side panels to each end of the second divider.

d. Press the seam allowances* open.

e. Place the dividers, with the side panels attached, Right sides together, matching the long edges. Pin the top and bottom edges of the divider together. Stitch a ½" seam across the top and bottom edges, starting and stopping at the seam that attaches the lining side panels. Backstitch at each end. Turn the divider Right side out.

f. Fold the lining side panels back onto the divider with the Right sides together. Match the ½" left unstitched at the top and bottom of the seam that attaches the divider. Pin in place. Stitch a ½" seam, ½" in length at the top and bottom of existing seam. Press the seam allowance open. Repeat this step on the opposite end of the divider, stitching the top and bottom of that seam.

g. Place the side panels Wrong sides together, matching the seams. Pin in place. Stitch-in-the-ditch* on the seam at one end of the divider to close the end. Backstitch at each end. Insert the Peltex panel inside the divider through the open end. Pin the open end closed, and stitch-in-the-ditch to enclose the Peltex.

h. Topstitch* a ½" seam across the top and bottom of the divider. Backstitch at each end.

Make and attach the inside pockets to the lining main panels. (FIGURE 2)

a. Find the center of each lining main panel and each pocket panel by folding them in half, matching short side edges. Gently press creases on the folded edges.

b. Place one interfaced pocket and one pocket without interfacing Right sides together. Pin across the long top edge. Stitch a ½" seam along the pinned edge, and backstitch at each end. Turn the pocket Right side out. Topstitch ½" from the top finished edge to create a casing for the elastic.

c. Attach the safety pin to one end of the first piece of elastic. Insert it into the casing from one end. Thread it through the casing and out the opposite end. Machine baste* across the ends of the elastic at each end of the casing.

d. Pin and machine baste the remaining three raw edges together.

e. Next, make pleats in the pockets. On bottom edge of the pocket, measure in from each side edge and make marks at 2 ½", 3 ½", 7 ½", and 8 ½". On the Right side of the pocket, fold the 3 ½" mark toward the 2 ½" mark. Pin and machine baste across the edge of the pleat. On the Right side of the pocket, fold the 7 ½" mark toward the 8 ½" mark. Pin and machine baste across the edge of the pleat. Repeat to make two pleats on the other end of the first pocket.

note: When basting the pleats, make sure the pleats on either side of the center crease face each other.

f. Repeat steps 4b through 4e to make the second pocket.

g. Place the back of the pocket on the Right side of the lining main panel, with the front of the pleats facing out. Match the side and bottom edges, and the center crease. Pin and machine baste the side and bottom edges.

h. Match the center crease on the pocket to the center crease on the lining main panel. Pin and then stitch along the matched center creases. Backstitch at each end.

i. Repeat steps 4g and 4h to attach the second pocket to the other lining main panel.

Attach the lining main and side panels.

a. Place the first lining main and side panels Right sides together. Pin the side edges. Stitch a ½" seam, stopping ½" from bottom edge, backstitching at each end.

b. Repeat to attach the opposite end of the first lining main panel to the second lining side panel.

c. Repeat to attach the second lining main panel to the remaining two lining side panels.

Attach the lining bottom panel to the lining main and side panels.

a. Place the bottom edge of the lining main panel and the long edge of the lining bottom panel Right sides together. Pin one long edge. Stitch a ½" seam, starting and stopping ½" from each end. Backstitch at each end.

b. Turn the lining at the side seam. Match the bottom edge of the lining side panel to the short end of the lining bottom panel. Pin. Stitch a ½" seam, starting and stopping ½" from each edge. Backstitch at each end.

c. Continue to turn the panels at the seams/corners, matching the edges. Stitch a ½" seam, backstitching at each end.

d. Trim* the corners in the seam allowance, being careful not to clip the stitching. Set the lining aside.

Make the side pockets, and sew them to the exterior side panels.

a. Place one side pocket panel with interfacing and one without interfacing Right sides together. Pin the short top edges. Stitch a ½" seam along the pinned edge. Backstitch at each end.

b. Turn the pocket Right side out, and press the seam. Topstitch ½" from the top finished edge. Pin and machine baste the three remaining edges.

c. Pin the side pocket to the exterior side panel, matching the bottom and side edges. Machine baste along the pinned edges.

d. Repeat steps 7a through 7c to make the second side pocket, and baste it to the second exterior side panel.

Figure 1.

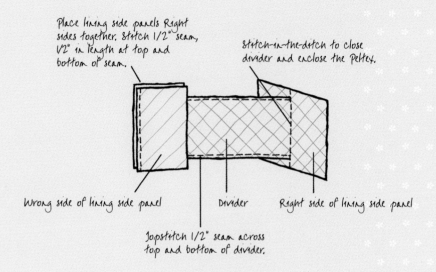

Place lining side panels Right sides together. Stitch 1/2" seam, 1/2" in length at top and bottom of seam.

Stitch-in-the-ditch to close divider and enclose the Peltex.

Wrong side of lining side panel

Divider

Right side of lining side panel

Topstitch 1/2" seam across top and bottom of divider.

Figure 2.

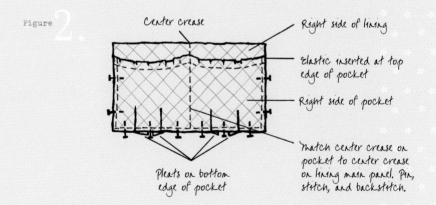

Center crease

Right side of lining

Elastic inserted at top edge of pocket

Right side of pocket

Match center crease on pocket to center crease on lining main panel. Pin, stitch, and backstitch.

Pleats on bottom edge of pocket

• STEP 8 •
Attach the exterior main and side panels.

Repeat step 5.

• STEP 9 •
Attach the exterior bottom panel to the exterior main and side panels.

Repeat step 6.

• STEP 10 •
Make and attach the strap*.

a. Using the first strap piece with interfacing attached, make a strap following instructions on page 172.

b. Repeat to make the second strap.

c. Measure 5" in from both side edges along the top edge of one exterior main panel, and mark. Repeat for the other exterior main panel.

d. Place the short end of the first strap to the inside of the first mark on one exterior main panel. Pin it in place. Place the other end of strap to the inside of the second mark. Do not twist the strap. Pin and machine baste the ends of the strap in place.

e. Repeat steps 10c and 10d to attach the second strap to the other exterior main panel.

• STEP 11 •
Attach the exterior and the lining. (FIGURE 3)

a. Turn the exterior Right side out. Use a turning tool* to push out the corners. Press along each seam.

b. Fold the top edge of the exterior ½" toward the Wrong side, and press. Repeat to fold the top edge of the lining.

c. With the Right side of the exterior and the Wrong side of the lining facing out, slip the lining inside the exterior. Match the top folded edges and pin them together. Edge stitch* completely around the top edges of the bag, backstitching at each end.

d. Beginning on one side of the divider, stitch 1" from the top edge, stopping at the divider on the opposite end of the bag. Backstitch at each end.

e. Begin again on the other side of the divider. Stitch 1" from the top edge on this side, stopping at the divider on the end where you first started stitching. Backstitch at each end.

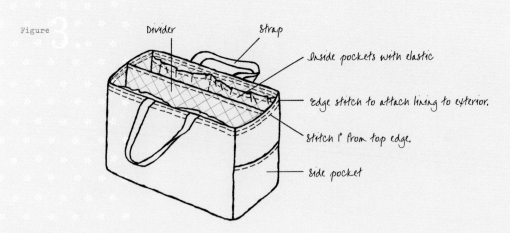

Figure 3

Divider

Strap

Inside pockets with elastic

Edge stitch to attach lining to exterior.

Stitch 1" from top edge.

Side pocket

k.

modern Diaper Bag WITH CHANGING PAD

bag finished size: 26 ½" wide at top, 18" wide across bottom, 26 ½" tall (with straps) x 4" deep
changing pad finished size: 18" wide x 24" long
difficulty level: 4

This modern design doesn't sacrifice much-needed space and interior pockets.
It even has a cell phone pocket on the exterior. The roll-up changing pad tucks inside;
a snap enclosure holds it all together.

FABRICS

For Diaper Bag

* 1 ¼ yards (44" or 54" wide)
mid-weight fabric for the exterior

* 1 ⅞ yards (44" or 54" wide)
mid-weight fabric for the lining

For Changing Pad

* ¾ yard (44" or 54" wide)
mid-weight print for the exterior

* ¾ yard (44" wide) coordinating
solid-color terry cloth

OTHER SUPPLIES

For Diaper Bag

* 2 ½ yards (44" wide) fusible fleece
(we use Fusible Thermolam Plus by Pellon)

* 3 yards (22" wide) mid-weight woven
fusible interfacing (we use SF101 by Pellon)

* ¼ yard (22" wide) single-sided fusible
Peltex or a similar heavy-weight stabilizer

* 1 magnetic closure, ¾" wide

* Pressing cloth

* 1 spool coordinating all-purpose
thread (we use Coats Dual Duty Plus)

For Changing Pad

* ¾ yard (60" wide) cotton batting

* 1" (¾" wide) sew-on Velcro

* 1 small spool coordinating all-purpose
thread (we use Coats Dual Duty Plus)

diaper bag

• STEP 1 •
Cut out the pattern pieces.

From the pattern sheet included with this book, cut out:

- Main panel
- Front closure

• STEP 2 •
Cut out all of the pieces from the fabric.

a. Place the pattern pieces on the fold of the fabric, and measure and mark the dimensions directly onto the Right side of the fabric. Cut along the marked lines.

b. From the exterior fabric, cut:

- 2 main panels on the fold (see General Notes, page 13)
- 2 front closures on the fold
- 2 side panels, each 5" wide x 13 ½" long
- 1 bottom panel, 5" wide x 19" long
- 2 straps, each 3" wide x 19" long
- 2 cell phone pockets, each 5 ¼" wide x 5 ½" long

c. From the lining fabric, cut:

- 2 main panels on the fold
- 2 side panels, each 5" wide x 13 ½" long
- 1 bottom panel, 5" wide x 19" long
- 4 inside long pockets, each 23" wide x 10" long
- 2 straps, each 3" wide x 19" long
- 4 bottle pockets, each 7" wide x 10" long

d. From the fusible fleece, cut:

- 4 main panels on the fold
- 1 front closure on the fold
- 4 side panels, each 5" wide x 13 ½" long
- 2 bottom panels, each 5" wide x 19" long
- 4 straps, each 3" wide x 19" long
- 1 cell phone pocket, 5 ¼" wide x 5 ½" long
- 2 bottle pockets, 7" wide x 10" long

e. From the fusible interfacing, cut:

- 2 main panels on the fold
- 1 front closure on the fold
- 2 side panels, each 5" wide x 13 ½" long
- 1 bottom panel, 5" wide x 19" long
- 2 inside long pockets, each 23" wide x 10" long

f. From fusible Peltex, cut:

- 2 bottom panels, each 4" wide x 18" long

• STEP 3 •

Attach the interfacings.

a. Place the Wrong side of both exterior main panels, both exterior side panels, 1 front closure, and 2 inside long pockets on the fusible side of the corresponding interfacing pieces. Use a pressing cloth* and follow the manufacturer's instructions to fuse the interfacing to the fabric.

b. Place the Wrong side of all 4 main panels, the side panels and straps, the bottom panel lining, the other front closure, 2 bottle pockets, and 1 cell phone pocket on top of the fusible side of the corresponding fleece pieces. Use a pressing cloth and follow the manufacturer's instructions to fuse the fleece to the fabric.

c. Place the fusible sides of the Peltex bottom panels together matching the outside edges. Fuse the Peltex in place.

d. Center the Peltex panels on the Wrong side of the exterior bottom panel. Place the interfacing, fusible-side down, on top of the Peltex, matching the edges of the panels. Using a pressing cloth, fuse the interfacing to the Peltex and around the edges of the bottom panel.

• STEP 4 •

Prepare the lining and pockets. (FIGURE 1)

a. Find the center of both lining main panels by folding them in half, matching the short edges. Gently press the fold to create a center crease. Repeat with each long pocket panel.

b. On the Right side of the first lining main panel, mark two lines running parallel to the center crease. One should be 9" to the left of the crease, and the other 9" to the right. They will be guides for placing the pockets.

c. Repeat to mark the lines on the other lining main panel.

• STEP 5 •

Attach the lining main and side panels. (FIGURE 1)

a. With Right sides together, match the edges of the lining's first main and side panels. Pin the side edges in place.

b. Sew a ½" seam down the edge, stopping ½" from the bottom edge, backstitching* at each end.

c. Sew the second side panel to the other end of the first main panel in the same way.

d. Repeat to attach the second main panel to the opposite edges of each side panel. Set aside.

• STEP 6 •

Make the interior pockets.

a. Place one interfaced bottle pocket piece and one long pocket piece Right sides together. Match the short side edges and pin them in place. Sew a ½" seam, stopping ½" from the bottom edge, backstitching at each end. Stitch the second interfaced bottle pocket piece to the other side of the first long pocket in the same way.

b. Repeat step 6a to attach the second interfaced long pocket to the opposite edges of each bottle pocket. You now have a circle of pocket pieces: long pocket, bottle, long pocket, bottle.

c. Press all seam allowances* open.

d. Repeat steps 6a through 6c with the other bottle and long pocket pieces to make the pocket's lining. You should now have two circles of pockets: one interfaced, the other not.

e. Place the Right sides of the pockets and the pocket lining together, matching the seams and the top edge, and pin in place. Stitch a ½" seam all the way around the top edge, backstitching at each end.

f. Flip the lining over the pocket, so the Wrong sides are together. Line up the bottom edges, and pin them together. Press the top seam flat. Topstitch* a ½" seam around the top edges. Machine baste* a ¼" seam around the bottom edges.

• STEP 7 •

Make the pleats on all the pockets.

a. Starting at the bottom edge of one long pocket, use a chalk pencil and ruler to measure and mark 4" in from each side seam. Make two more marks, each 4" from the center crease, one on either side of it. Repeat to mark the pleats on the other long pocket.

b. On the bottom edge of each bottle pocket, measure and mark 2" in from each side seam.

c. Fold the first long pocket, Right sides together, at each mark to form a box pleat. Pin in place. Sew a 1" seam, ½" from, and parallel to, the folded edge, backstitching at each end.

d. Press the pleat that forms on the back of the pockets toward the center of the panel. Machine baste ¼" from bottom edge across each pleat.

e. Repeat steps 7c and 7d to make the pleats on the other long pocket and both bottle pockets.

• STEP 8 •

Attach the pockets to the lining. (FIGURE 2)

a. Place the lining side of the first long pocket on the Right side of the lining main panel, matching the center creases. Pin them together at the crease.

b. Match the seams on the pocket to the guidelines you drew in step 4b. Pin down both side seams. Stitch the pockets to the main panel down both seams and at the center crease, backstitching at each end.

c. Repeat to attach the second long pocket to the other lining main panel.

d. Match the bottom edges of the pockets to the bottom edge of the bag. Pin and machine baste a ¼" seam all the way around the bottom edges.

• STEP 9 •

Attach the bottom panel to the lining.

a. Place the bottom edge of the lining main panel and the long edge of the bottom panel Right sides together. Pin them in place.

b. Sew a ½" seam across the long edge, starting and stopping ½" from each edge, backstitching at each end.

c. Turn the panel at the seam, matching the bottom edge of the side panel with the short end of the bottom panel. Pin them in place.

d. Continue to turn the panels at the seams, matching the edges, and stitching them together. Backstitch at each end.

e. Trim* the corner in the seam allowance, making sure not to clip the stitching.

• STEP 10 •

Attach the strap to the lining.

a. Place one short end of the strap and the top of the lining main panel Right sides together. Pin in place. Sew a seam ½" from the edge, and backstitch at each end. Press the seam allowance open. Topstitch ½" on each side of the seam.

b. Repeat, attaching the other end of the strap to the other top edge of the main panel.

c. Repeat steps 10a and 10b to attach the other strap on the other lining main panel. Set the lining aside.

• STEP 11 •

Make four darts on the cell phone pocket.

a. Using a chalk pencil and ruler, measure and mark 2" in from each side, along the top and bottom edges on both cell phone pocket panels.

b. Fold the interfaced pocket panel Right sides together at the first 2" mark. Pin in place. Measure 1 ½" down along the folded edge, and mark on the Wrong side. Starting ⅜" from the folded edge at the top of the pocket, stitch at an angle to the 1 ½" mark you just made, backstitching at each end.

c. Repeat to make the other top dart on the interfaced pocket panel and two darts along the bottom edge.

d. Repeat to make all four darts on the second phone pocket panel, which will be used for the pocket lining.

• STEP 12 •

Make the cell phone pocket.

a. Place the exterior and lining cell phone pocket panels Right sides together. Match the darts, and pin the edges in place.

b. Stitch a ½" seam around the edges, leaving a 2 ½" opening on one long side edge, backstitching at each end.

c. Trim the corners in the seam allowance, making sure not to clip the stitching.

d. Turn the pocket Right side out, using a turning tool* to push out the corners and press. Fold ½" under on both the exterior and lining at the opening. Pin in place. (The opening will be stitched closed when the pocket is attached.)

e. Topstitch a ½" seam across the top edge, backstitching at each end.

• STEP 13 •

Attach the cell phone pocket to the exterior side panel.

a. Measure and mark 2" down from each end of the top edge of the first side panel. Draw a guideline between the two marks. Measure and mark 1" in from each side on the guideline.

b. Place the top of the pocket along the guideline, and each side of the pocket at the 1" marks. Pin the sides and bottom edge in place. (The pocket stands out from the side panel.)

c. Edge stitch* down both sides and across the bottom of the pocket, backstitching at each end.

• STEP 14 •

Attach the magnetic snap.

a. Find the center of the main panel by folding it in half lengthwise. Gently press the fold to form a crease.

b. Measure and mark 3" down from the top edge on the center crease.

c. Center the female half of the magnetic snap below the 3" mark and over the crease. Follow the manufacturer's instructions to attach the snap.

d. Find the center of the front closure lining by folding it in half lengthwise. Gently press a center crease on the folded edge.

e. Measure and mark 1" up from the bottom edge on the center crease.

f. Center the male half of the magnetic snap above the 1" mark and over the crease. Follow the manufacturer's instructions to attach the snap.

• STEP 15 •

Attach the exterior main and side panels together.

Repeat step 5, using the exterior pieces. First decide on which side of the bag you will want to attach the side panel with the cell phone pocket; it should be on the side of the bag that will be carried toward your front.

• STEP 16 •

Attach the bottom panel to the exterior.

Repeat step 9, using the exterior pieces.

• STEP 17 •

Attach the strap to the exterior main panel.

Repeat step 10, using the exterior pieces.

• STEP 18 •

Turn the exterior of the bag Right side out.

Use a turning tool to push out the corners. Press along each seam. Set aside.

• STEP 19 •

Make the front closure.

a. Place the front closure pieces Right sides together, and pin in place. Stitch a ½" seam down the long sides and around the bottom curve. Trim the corners in the seam allowance, and clip the seam allowance around the curve every ½" to ¾". Make sure not to clip the stitching.

b. Turn the closure Right side out, pushing out the corners, and press. Topstitch ¼" from the finished edges, backstitching at each end.

• STEP 20 •

Attach the front closure to the exterior back main panel. (FIGURE 3)

a. Place the front closure and back main panel Right sides together. Match the center creases and raw edges. The magnetic snap should face out. Pin together.

b. Machine baste a ¼" seam across the matched edges.

• STEP 21 •

Sew the exterior and lining together. (FIGURE 3)

a. With the Right side of the exterior and the Wrong side of the lining facing out, slip the lining over the exterior and pin the top and outside edge of the strap in place.

b. Stitch a ½" seam around the outside edges of the main panels and strap, backstitching at each end. (The inside edges of the handle opening are left open and will be stitched closed in step 23.)

• STEP 22 •

Finish the outside edges. (FIGURE 3)

a. Turn the bag Right side out through one of the handle openings, pushing the lining down inside. Use a turning tool to push out the corners. Press.

b. Edge stitch around the outside finished edges, and back-stitch at each end.

• STEP 23 •

Finish the top opening on the main panel and the inner edge of the strap. (FIGURE 3)

a. Sew a ½" stay-stitching* line around each strap's unfinished edges, and on the rest of opening on the main panel.

b. Clip into the seam allowance at each angled corner on the main panel, being careful not to clip the stitching.

c. Fold all the unfinished edges on the panels and strap ½" under. Pin together.

d. Edge stitch completely around the matched edges on the front and back of the bag, including the strap, backstitching at each end. (The front closure is attached to the back of bag.)

e. Press the bag completely.

Figure 1.

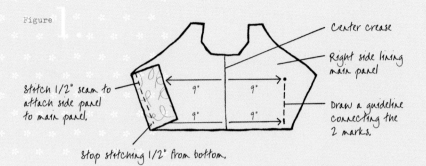

Center crease

Right side lining main panel

Draw a guideline connecting the 2 marks.

Stitch 1/2" seam to attach side panel to main panel.

9"   9"

9"   9"

Stop stitching 1/2" from bottom.

Figure 2.

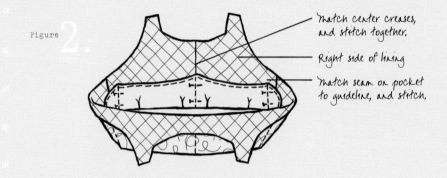

match center creases, and stitch together.

Right side of lining

match seam on pocket to guideline, and stitch.

Figure 3.

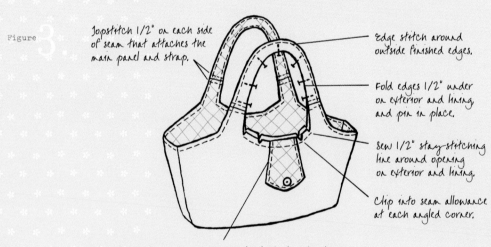

Topstitch 1/2" on each side of seam that attaches the main panel and strap.

Edge stitch around outside finished edges.

Fold edges 1/2" under on exterior and lining and pin in place.

Sew 1/2" stay-stitching line around opening on exterior and lining.

Clip into seam allowance at each angled corner.

Place front closure and back panel Right sides together.

changing pad

• STEP 1 •

Cut out all of the pieces from the fabric.

Measure and mark the dimensions directly onto the Right side of the fabric. Cut along the marked lines.

a. From the exterior fabric, cut:

- 1 back panel: 19" wide x 25" long
- 1 strap: 4" wide x 12" long

b. From the terry cloth, cut:

- 1 front panel: 19" wide x 25" long

c. From the batting, cut:

- 2 panels: 21" wide x 27" long

• STEP 2 •

Mark the quilting guidelines.

a. On the Right side of the back panel, measure and mark across the top and bottom edges at 3 ½", 6 ½", 9 ½", 12 ½", and 15 ½". Measure and mark down both the side edges at 3 ½", 6 ½", 9 ½", 12 ½", 15 ½", 18 ½", and 21 ½".

b. Draw lines connecting the vertical and horizontal marks to form a grid.

• STEP 3 •

Make the strap*.

Follow the instructions on page 172 to make the strap.

• STEP 4 •

Attach Velcro to the strap.

a. Measure and mark 1 ½" from the raw end of the strap. Center a 1" piece of male Velcro to the inside of the mark. Pin it in place. Edge stitch completely around the Velcro, backstitching at each end.

b. Turn the strap over. Center a 1" piece of female Velcro ⅛" from the finished end of the strap. Pin it in place. Edge stitch completely around the Velcro, backstitching at each end.

• STEP 5 •

Attach the strap to the back panel.

Place the strap so the male Velcro faces the back panel. Center the raw end over the 9 ½" vertical quilting guideline on the short end of the pad. Pin it in place. Machine baste a ¼" seam across the end of the strap.

• STEP 6 •

Assemble the Changing Pad.

a. Center the Wrong side of the back panel on top of the two batting panels. Pin them in place. Machine baste a ¼" seam all the way around the back panel.

b. Trim the batting even with the back panel.

c. Place the front and back panels Right sides together. Pin in place. Stitch a ½" seam around the edges, leaving a 4" opening centered on one edge, backstitching at each end.

d. Trim the corners in the seam allowance, making sure not to clip the stitching.

e. Turn the pad Right side out, use a turning tool to push out the corners, and press. Fold ½" under on each side of the opening, and pin in place. Edge stitch completely around the outside edge of the pad, backstitching at each end. Press it flat.

• STEP 7 •

Quilt the Changing Pad.

a. First pin the back to the front panel along the quilting guidelines.

b. On the Right side of the back panel, starting on the center vertical line, stitch along the guideline, backstitching at each end. Continue stitching along all the vertical guidelines from the center out.

c. Repeat the above step to stitch the horizontal guidelines, backstitching at each end. Trim the excess threads, and press.

chapter: 5.0 baby decor

* PATCHWORK CRIB/PLAYTIME QUILT * CHEEKY MONKEY LAUNDRY BAG
* SLEEPY SNAIL WITH REMOVABLE SHELL PILLOW * QUICK-CHANGE TABLETOP SET

the everyday things of baby's little world should be fresh and fun. A nice baby's room is stimulating for the little one and enjoyable for you, too. A pretty patchwork crib quilt is a simple design with multiple uses. A handy tabletop changing pad is another example of utility made beautiful. A saucy monkey laundry bag and a sleepy snail keep the adorable (and the humor) present throughout baby's day.

1.

DIFFICULTY LEVEL *2

PATCHWORK CRIB/PLAYTIME QUILT ⇒

instructions: P.116

DIFFICULTY LEVEL 3^*

m.

CHEEKY MONKEY LAUNDRY BAG ⟹

instructions: P.119

n.

DIFFICULTY LEVEL *3*

SLEEPY SNAIL WITH REMOVABLE SHELL PILLOW ⟹   instructions: _P.124_

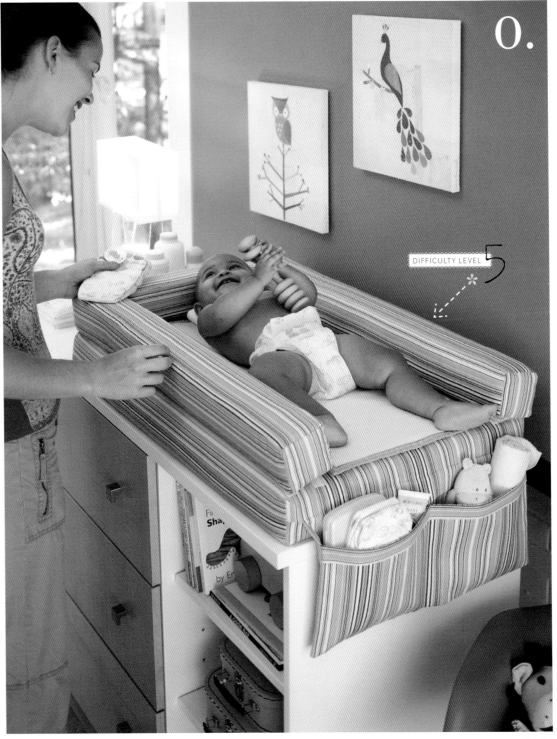

O.

DIFFICULTY LEVEL 5

QUICK-CHANGE TABLETOP SET ⇒

instructions: P.128

1.

patchwork crib/playtime quilt

finished size: 34" wide x 44" long
difficulty level: 2

This patchwork quilt is great for cuddle- and playtime. And, it folds or rolls up neatly for carrying and storing. The perfect gift for growing babies, it can be personalized with your choices of fabrics. Match baby's room or mix and match vintage and contemporary prints.

FABRICS

* ⅞ yard (44" or 54" wide) each of two different mid-weight prints for the front (prints A and B)
* ½ yard (44" or 54" wide) each of two different mid-weight prints for the front (prints C and D)
* 2 ¼ yards (44" or 54" wide) coordinating mid-weight fabric for back and binding

OTHER SUPPLIES

* 1 crib-size package batting (we use Fairfield Poly-fil Hi-Loft Batting)
* 1 large spool coordinating all-purpose thread (we use Coats Dual Duty Plus)
* Long hand-sewing needle or large safety pins, and contrasting thread for basting
* Walking or quilting foot for sewing machine (optional; see Note)
* Masking tape (optional)

NOTE

* A walking foot (or an even-feed foot) for your sewing machine can reduce puckering on the quilt back but is not necessary.

• STEP 1 •
Cut out all of the pieces from the fabric.

a. Using a chalk pencil and ruler, measure and mark the dimensions directly onto the Right side of the fabric. Cut along the marked lines, and organize them by print and size. Bias binding* will be cut in Step 7 from the remaining backing fabric.

b. From print A, cut:
- 16 pieces, each 5 ¼" wide x 6 ½" long (for block #2)
- 4 strips, each 2" wide x 12" long (for block #1)
- 4 strips, each 2 ¼" wide x 12" long (for block #3)

c. From print B, cut:
- 16 pieces, each 5 ¼" wide x 6 ½" long (for block #2)
- 4 strips, each 3" wide x 12" long (for block #1)
- 4 strips, each 2 ½" wide x 12" long (for block #3)

d. From print C, cut:
- 4 strips, each 3 ¾" wide x 12" long (for block #1)
- 4 strips, each 4 ¼" wide x 12" long (for block #3)

e. From print D, cut:
- 4 strips, each 3 ¾" wide x 12" long (for block #1)
- 4 strips, each 3 ½" wide x 12" long (for block #3)

f. From the backing fabric, cut:
- 1 piece 38" wide x 48" long

g. From the batting, cut:
- 1 piece 38" wide x 48" long

Piece the blocks together. (FIGURE 1)

a. Make block #1:

- Place a 3 ¾" strip of print C and a 2" strip of print A Right sides together. Pin one long edge. Stitch a ½" seam along the pinned edge, backstitching* at each end.
- Place a 3" strip of print B Right sides together with the attached strip of print A. Pin the long edges. Stitch a ½" seam along the pinned edge, backstitching at each end.
- Place a 3 ¾" strip of print D Right sides together with the attached strip of print B. Pin the long edges. Stitch a ½" seam along the pinned edge, backstitching at each end.
- Press all of the seam allowances* to one side.
- Repeat to make three additional block #1s.

b. Make block #2:

- Place a 5 ¼" x 6 ½" piece of prints A and B Right sides together. Pin one long edge. Stitch a ½" seam along the pinned edge, backstitching at each end.
- Repeat to make a second set of prints A and B.
- Place the two sets Right sides together, placing like prints diagonally. Pin the long seamed edge. Stitch a ½" seam along the pinned edge, backstitching at each end.
- Press all of the seam allowances to one side.
- Repeat to make seven additional block #2s.

c. Make block #3:

- Place a 4 ¼" strip of print C and a 2 ¼" strip of print A Right sides together. Pin one long edge. Stitch a ½" seam along the pinned edge, backstitching at each end.
- Place a 3 ½" strip of print D Right sides together with the attached strip of print A. Pin the long edge. Stitch a ½" seam along the pinned edge, backstitching at each end.
- Place a 2 ½" strip of print B Right sides together with the attached strip of print D. Pin the long edge. Stitch a ½" seam along the pinned edge, backstitching at each end.
- Press all of the seam allowances to one side.
- Repeat to make three additional block #3s.

Lay out the blocks, and stitch them together.

a. Arrange the finished blocks on a flat surface in this order:

- Row 1 (top) #1, #2, #3, #2
- Row 2 #2, #3, #2, #1
- Row 3 #3, #2, #1, #2
- Row 4 #2, #1, #2, #3

b. Begin at the upper left corner. Place a block #1 and a block #2 Right sides together. Match one long raw edge, and pin in place. Stitch a ½" seam along the pinned edge, backstitching each end.

c. Place a block #3 Right sides together with the attached block #2. Match the long raw edges, and pin them in place. Stitch a ½" seam along the pinned edge, backstitching each end.

d. Place a second block #2 Right sides together with the attached block #3. Match the long raw edges, and pin them in place. Stitch a ½" seam along the pinned edge, backstitching each end.

e. Press all of the seam allowances to one side.

f. Repeat this process to attach the blocks in the second row. Press the seam allowances in the opposite direction from those in row 1. Again, repeat the process to attach the blocks in the third row. Press the seam allowances in the same direction as row 1. Finally, repeat the process to attach the blocks in the bottom row. Press the seam allowances in the same direction as row 2.

Attach the rows together.

a. Place row 1 and row 2 Right sides together. Match the bottom long edge of row 1 to the top long edge of row 2. Match the seams between the blocks. Pin the rows together. Stitch a ½" seam along the pinned edge, backstitching at each end.

b. Repeat to attach the top edge of row 3 to the bottom edge of row 2, and the top edge of row 4 to the bottom edge of row 3.

c. Press all of the seam allowances toward the bottom.

Assemble the Quilt.

a. Place the quilt back Wrong side up on a large, flat surface, and smooth out the wrinkles. You may find it helpful to tape the edges to the flat surface to keep it in place while basting.

b. Place the batting on top of the back. Smooth out any wrinkles.

c. Center the quilt front, Right side up, on top of the batting.

d. Hand-baste* the three layers together with contrasting thread, using long basting stitches, or pin the three layers together with large safety pins.

Quilt the Quilt.

a. Stitch-in-the-ditch* along all the seam lines, backstitching at each end. Begin stitching at the center of the quilt and work toward the edges.

b. Roll up the excess quilt not being stitched, as you sew, to reduce weight.

c. Trim the edges of the backing and batting even with the quilt front.

Cut, prepare, and apply the bias binding*.

Refer to Glossary and Techniques (page 169). Cut and prepare the French bias binding: strips should be 3 ¼" wide, and you'll need a total of 175" in length. Attach the bias binding to the front of the quilt using a ½" seam, and miter* the corners. Stitch the binding to the back.

Figure 1

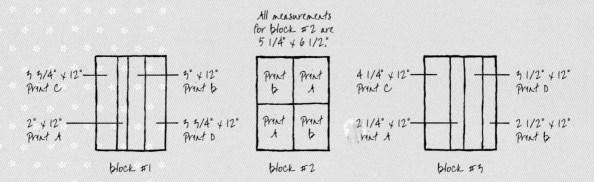

3 3/4" x 12" Print C — 3" x 12" Print B
2" x 12" Print A — 3 3/4" x 12" Print D
block #1

All measurements for block #2 are 5 1/4" x 6 1/2".
Print B | Print A
Print A | Print B
block #2

4 1/4" x 12" Print C — 3 1/2" x 12" Print D
2 1/4" x 12" Print A — 2 1/2" x 12" Print B
block #3

m.

CHEEKY MONKEY LAUNDRY BAG

finished size: 18" wide x 25" tall (plus tail)
difficulty level: 3

You won't be able to resist the Cheeky Monkey. This cute character will help you find the humor in the most daunting of chores. Machine washable, it has an easy front opening and a design that allows you to hang it on a crib, door, or wall hook for quick access.

FABRICS

* 2 ¼ yards (44" wide) light- to mid-weight fabric or 1 ⅝ yards (54" wide) heavier home-decorating fabric for the exterior, lining, and drawstrings

* ½ yard (44" wide) brown fabric for the monkey's body, head, outer ears, and tail

* 4" x 9" piece white or ivory fabric for the mouth, inner ears, and feet

OTHER SUPPLIES

* 1 ½ yards (20" wide) mid-weight woven fusible interfacing (we use SF101 by Pellon)

* ½ yard (17" wide) Wonder-Under or similar fusible webbing for the mouth and body

* 12" (¾" wide) sew-on Velcro

* 1 spool coordinating all-purpose thread (we use Coats Dual Duty Plus)

* 1 bag (12 oz.) Nature-fil (all-natural premium fiberfill by Fairfield)

* Wax-free tracing paper by Prym-Dritz

* Tracing wheel

* 1 skein black perle cotton embroidery floss for the face details

* Tapestry needle (size 20 or 22)

* Large safety pin

• STEP 1 •

Cut out the monkey pattern pieces.

From the pattern sheet included with this book, cut out:

- Tail
- Feet
- Head
- Body
- Inner ear
- Outer ear
- Mouth

• STEP 2 •

Cut out all of the pieces from the fabric.

a. Use a chalk pencil and ruler to measure and mark the dimensions directly onto the Right side of the fabric. Cut along the marked lines.

b. From the exterior/lining print, cut:

- 2 back panels, each 19" wide x 26" long
- 4 front panels, each 10" wide x 26" long
- 4 drawstring strips, each 4" wide x 22 ½" long

c. Fold the brown fabric Wrong sides together, and cut:

- 2 heads
- 2 tails
- 4 outer ears

d. Follow the manufacturer's instructions to apply Wonder-Under to the Wrong side of a single layer of the remaining brown fabric. Place the body pattern Right side down on the Wonder-Under. Trace around the pattern. Cut:

- 1 body

e. Follow the manufacturer's instructions to apply Wonder-Under to the Wrong side of a single layer of white or ivory fabric. Place the pattern pieces Right side down on the Wonder-Under. Trace around the pattern. Cut:

- 1 mouth
- 2 inner ears
- 2 feet

f. From the fusible interfacing, cut:

- 1 back panel, 19" wide x 26" long
- 2 front panels, each 10" wide x 26" long

g. From the Velcro, cut:

- 1 strip, 6 ½" long
- 1 strip, 5" long

Trim the female pieces to 4" long.

· STEP 3 ·

Apply the interfacing.

a. Place the first back panel Right side up on the fusible side of the interfacing. Follow the manufacturer's instructions to fuse them together, using an iron's "wool" setting.

b. Repeat to attach the interfacing to the two remaining front exterior panels.

· STEP 4 ·

Make the exterior front.

a. Place the two front panels Right sides together. Pin one long edge. To make an opening for laundry, measure down the pinned edge to 5" and 15" from the top. Make marks at these spots.

b. Stitch a ½" seam along the pinned edge. Begin at the top and stitch to the 5" mark, backstitching* at each end. Start again at the 15" mark and stitch to the bottom, backstitching at each end. Leave the 10" opening unstitched.

c. Press the seam allowance* open.

· STEP 5 ·

Apply the monkey body to the bag's front.

a. Remove the Wonder-Under backing from the feet. Follow the manufacturer's instructions to fuse the feet to the Right side of the monkey's body. Remove the Wonder-Under backing from the body. Machine satin stitch* the feet to the legs using a short zigzag stitch across the top edge of the feet.

b. Place the body on the bottom of the exterior front panel's Right side. Place the long, straight edge even with the bag's bottom. The monkey's neck should be 1" from the right raw edge of the panel.

c. Fuse the body to the panel. Machine satin stitch around the body. Do not stitch across the body's long straight edge.

· STEP 6 ·

Make the monkey's tail.

a. Place the tail pieces Right sides together. Pin the outer edges. Use a short stitch to sew a ½" seam around the outer edges, backstitching at each end. Leave the short, straight end open.

b. Trim the tail's seam allowance to ¼".

c. Turn the tail Right side out and stuff it firmly with fiberfill, leaving 1" at the open end unstuffed. Stitch a ½" seam across the short open end, backstitching at each end.

· STEP 7 ·

Attach the tail, and complete the exterior. (FIGURE 1)

a. On the front, lower right corner, measure up 2 ½" from the corner. Make a mark. Measure 2 ½" across the bottom edge from the right corner. Make a mark.

b. Place the bottom edge of the 5" strip of male Velcro diagonally between marks. Pin and stitch it in place, backstitching at each end. Place the 6 ½" strip of male Velcro ¼" above the first piece. Pin and stitch it in place, backstitching at each end. Trim the ends of the Velcro even with the sides of the front panel.

c. Place the tail at the left bottom edge, 1" in from the edge of the body, curling toward the outer edge. Pin the tail in place, and machine baste* it to the panel.

d. Place the front and back panels Right sides together. Match the raw side and bottom edges. Pin together.

e. Make a mark 1 ½" down from the top, along both sides. Make another mark at 2 ½" from the top on both sides. (These marks indicate where the drawstring openings will be.)

f. Stitch a ½" seam, starting at the top edge, and stopping at the 1 ½" mark. Begin stitching again at the 2 ½" mark. Stitch down the side, across the bottom, and up the second side, stopping at the 2 ½" mark. Begin stitching again at the 1 ½" mark, and stitch to the top edge, backstitching at each end. Stitch a second time over the tail to strengthen the stitching.

g. Trim* the corners in the seam allowances, making sure not to clip the stitching. Press the seam allowances open.

h. Turn the bag Right side out. Push out the corners using a turning tool*.

• STEP 8 •

Make the lining.

a. Repeat step 4 to attach the front lining panels.

b. Place the front and back panels Right sides together. Pin the side and bottom edges.

c. Stitch a ½" seam down each side and across the bottom, backstitching at each end.

• STEP 9 •

Attach the lining to the exterior.

a. Turn the exterior Right side out and the lining Wrong side out. Slide the lining over the exterior. Match and pin the side and front seams and the top raw edges.

b. Stitch a ½" seam around the top edge, and backstitch at each end.

c. Turn the bag Right side out through the front opening, and push the lining down inside the exterior. Press the top edge.

d. Edge stitch* completely around the top, backstitching at each end.

• STEP 10 •

Make the casing for the drawstring. (FIGURE 2)

a. Pin the exterior and lining together and stitch 1" from the top, completely around the top edge, backstitching at each end.

b. Stitch 2" from the top, completely around the top edge, backstitching at each end.

• STEP 11 •

Attach the exterior and lining at the front opening.
(FIGURE 2)

a. Match the folded edges at both front openings, the lining to the exterior. Pin.

b. Edge stitch around the front opening, stitching down one side, across the bottom, up the second side, and across the top. Backstitch at each end.

• STEP 12 •

Make the monkey's head.

a. Make the ears: (FIGURE 3)

- Remove the Wonder-Under paper backing from the inner ear. Transfer the ear placement lines from the pattern piece to the Right side of each front ear, using tracing paper* and a tracing wheel* or a chalk pencil. Fuse the inner ear in place on the Right side of each front outer ear.
- Machine satin-stitch around the outer edge of the inner ear.
- Place the outer ear's front and back Right sides together. Pin.
- Stitch a ½" seam, using small stitches, around the outer edges, leaving the bottom edges open. Backstitch at each end.
- Trim the seam allowance to ¼".
- Turn the ear Right side out. Press.
- Stuff lightly with fiberfill, leaving 1" at the open end unstuffed.
- Machine baste the open end closed.

Figure 1.

Right side of front

Center seam

10" unstitched opening in seam

Monkey body and feet fused, then stitched to front.

6 1/2" male Velcro

5" male Velcro

2 1/2"

2 1/2"

1"

Stuffed tail placed 1" from left edge of monkey

Machine baste tail in place.

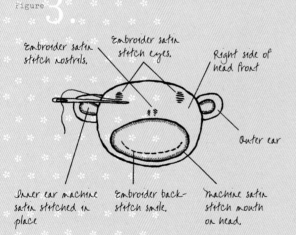

Figure 2.

Drawstring openings on each side

Stitch edges at 1" and 2" from top edge to form casing.

Stitch lining to front at the front opening.

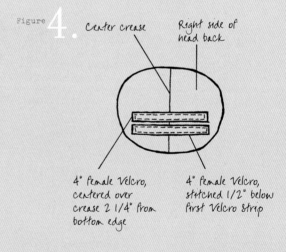

Figure 3.

Embroider satin stitch nostrils.

Embroider satin stitch eyes.

Right side of head front

Outer ear

Inner ear machine satin stitched in place

Embroider back-stitch smile.

Machine satin stitch mouth on head.

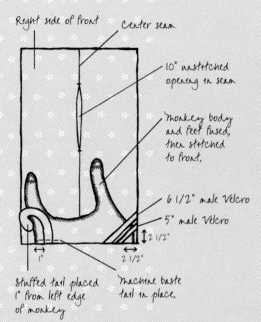

Figure 4.

Center crease

Right side of head back

4" female Velcro, centered over crease 2 1/4" from bottom edge

4" female Velcro, stitched 1/2" below first Velcro strip

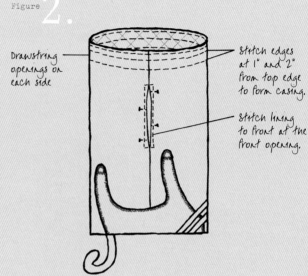

b. Make the head: (FIGURE 3)

- Transfer the marks for the face and ears from the pattern to the head-front.
- Remove the Wonder-Under backing from the mouth.
- Transfer the smile from the pattern to the mouth piece.
- Fuse the mouth to the head front.
- Machine satin stitch around the mouth.
- Embroider backstitch* the smile. Embroider satin stitch* the nostrils and eyes using perle cotton embroidery floss and a tapestry needle.*
- Place the ears on the head front at the placement marks, Right sides together, matching the raw edges. Pin and machine baste the ears in place.

c. Attach female Velcro to the head back. (FIGURE 4)

- Fold the head back in half lengthwise, and gently press a crease on the fold.
- Place the 4" female Velcro strip, centered over crease, with the bottom edge of the strip 2 ¼" from the bottom edge of the head back. Pin and stitch it in place, backstitching at each end.
- Place the second 4" strip of female Velcro ¼" below the first strip. Pin it in place and then sew it on, backstitching at each end.

d. Place the head front and back Right sides together, tucking the ears toward the face. Pin. Stitch around the head using small stitches, backstitching at each end. Leave a 3" opening at the bottom.

- Trim the seam allowance to ¼".
- Turn the head Right side out, and press.
- Stuff firmly with fiberfill.
- Turn under the seam allowance at the opening. Pin together, then slipstitch* the opening closed.

• STEP 13 •

Make and insert the drawstrings.

a. Place two drawstring strips Right sides together, matching all edges. Pin one of the short ends and stitch a ½" seam along the pinned edge, backstitching at each end. Press the seam allowance open.

b. Repeat to make the second drawstring piece.

c. Follow the instructions for making a strap on page 172 and make two drawstrings.

d. Attach the safety pin to one end of the first drawstring. Thread the pin through the right side opening through the casing, and out same opening. Remove the safety pin.

e. Repeat with the second drawstring, using the opening on the left side of the casing.

f. Tie the ends of the drawstrings together on each side of the bag.

g. Attach the monkey's head to the front of the bag using Velcro.

n.

sleepy snail WITH REMOVABLE SHELL PILLOW

finished size: 22" long x 12" tall x 10" wide
difficulty level: 3

This super cutie is a great toy, decoration, and cozy pillow all in one. The spiral ruffle "shell" pillows are removable for ease of washing or to use at naptime or playtime.

FABRICS

* ½ yard (44" or 54" wide) mid-weight solid for the snail's body (fabric A)

* ⅞ yard (44" or 54" wide) coordinating mid-weight print for the shell pillow panels and some of the snail's stripes (fabric B)

* 1 ⅛ yards (44" or 54" wide) coordinating mid-weight print for the ruffles on the shell pillows (fabric C)

* ¼ yard (44" or 54" wide) mid-weight print for snail's stripes (fabric D)

* ¼ yard (44" or 54" wide) mid-weight print for the remaining snail's stripes (fabric E)

OTHER SUPPLIES

* 18" (¾" wide) sew-on Velcro

* Tracing wheel and wax-free tracing paper by Prym-Dritz

* 1 spool coordinating all-purpose thread (we use Coats Dual Duty Plus)

* Tapestry needle (size 20 or 22) for stitching the eyes and mouth

* 1 skein coordinating perle cotton embroidery floss

* 2 bags (24 oz.) Nature-fil (all-natural premium fiberfill by Fairfield)

* Sharp hand-sewing needle

* Seam ripper

• STEP 1 •

Cut out the pattern pieces.

From the pattern sheet included with this book, cut out:

- Body
- Shell pillow panel

• STEP 2 •

Cut out all of the pieces from the fabric.

a. If fabric A is 54" wide, then fold it in half lengthwise with Wrong sides together, and cut two snail bodies using the pattern piece. If fabric A is 44" wide, then open up the fabric, and cut the front of the snail body by placing the pattern piece Right side up on the Right side of the fabric. Pin it in place, and cut around the outside edge of the pattern piece. Then flip the pattern piece over so the Right side of the pattern is facing the Right side of the fabric. Pin, and cut it out.

b. Use the pattern pieces, and measure and mark the following dimensions for the ruffle and stripes directly onto the Right side of the fabrics. Cut along the marked lines.

c. Fold fabric B in half lengthwise with Wrong sides together, cut:

- 4 shell pillow panels, using the provided pattern
- 2 snail stripes, each 1 ¼" wide x 7 ½" long
- 4 snail stripes, each 2 ¼" wide x 7 ½" long

d. From fabric C, cut:

- 4 ruffles, each 9 ½" wide x 40" long

e. From fabric D, cut:

- 4 snail stripes, each 1 ¾" wide x 7 ½" long
- 2 snail stripes, each 1 ¼" wide x 7 ½" long

f. From fabric E, cut:

- 2 snail stripes, each 2 ¼" wide x 7 ½" long
- 2 snail stripes, each 1 ¾" wide x 7 ½" long
- 2 snail stripes, each 1 ¼" wide x 7 ½" long

g. From the Velcro (male and female), cut:

- 1 piece, 4" long for the top back of the pillows
- 2 pieces, each 1" long for the front of the snail's body and the pillows
- 2 pieces, each 3 ½" long for the center of the snail's body and the pillows
- 2 pieces, each 2" long for the back of the snail's body and the pillows

h. Round the corners on the Velcro pieces as shown on the pattern.

• STEP 3 •

Transfer the marks* from the pattern to the fabric.

a. Using tracing paper*, a tracing wheel* or a chalk pencil, and the pattern piece as a guide:

- Transfer the marks on the Right side along the edges on the front and back of the snail body for stripe placement. Draw lines between the top and bottom marks.
- Transfer the Velcro placement marks onto the Right side of both snail bodies.
- Transfer the eyes and mouth onto the Right side of the front snail body.
- Transfer the ½" stitching line onto the Wrong side of the front snail body.

b. On first front pillow panel, transfer the swirl line for placing the ruffle. Transfer the swirl on the second front panel by flipping the pattern piece over so the writing side is facing the Right side of the fabric.

c. Transfer the Velcro placement lines to the first back pillow panel, using the pattern as a guide. Then transfer the Velcro placement lines to the second back panel by flipping the pattern piece over so the writing side is facing the Right side of the fabric.

• STEP 4 •

Make the stripes, and attach them to the body.
(FIGURE 1)

a. Fold each stripe's long edge ¼" in toward the Wrong side. Press. Place the stripes between the appropriate guidelines and pin them in place. Edge stitch* down both sides on each stripe, backstitching* at each end.

b. Trim the excess edges of each stripe so they are even with the edge of the snail's body.

• STEP 5 •

Make the snail's face. (FIGURE 1)

Using a tapestry needle and cotton perle, embroider satin stitch* the eyes and a mouth on the Right side of the snail's front.

• STEP 6 •

Attach the female Velcro to the snail's body. (FIGURE 1)

Pin the Velcro onto the front and back of the snail's body in the marked positions. Sew a large zigzag stitch completely around each Velcro piece, backstitching at each end.

• STEP 7 •

Sew the snail's body.

a. With Right sides together, match the stripes on the front and back of the snail. Pin them in place.

b. Sew a ½" seam around the edge, leaving a 3" opening on the belly for stuffing, backstitching at each end.

c. Trim the seam allowance to ¼" around the tight curves of the eyes and tail. Clip* into the seam allowance at the curves, making sure not to clip the stitching.

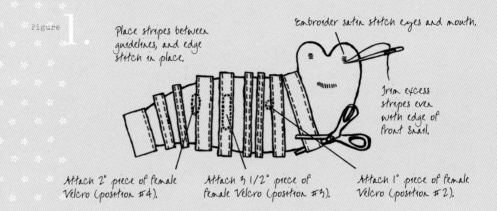

Figure 1.

Place stripes between guidelines, and edge stitch in place.

Embroider satin stitch eyes and mouth.

Trim excess stripes even with edge of front snail.

Attach 2" piece of female Velcro (position #4).

Attach 3 1/2" piece of female Velcro (position #3).

Attach 1" piece of female Velcro (position #2).

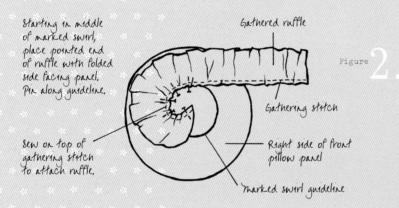

Figure 2.

Starting in middle of marked swirl, place pointed end of ruffle with folded side facing panel. Pin along guideline.

Gathered ruffle

Gathering stitch

Sew on top of gathering stitch to attach ruffle.

Right side of front pillow panel

Marked swirl guideline

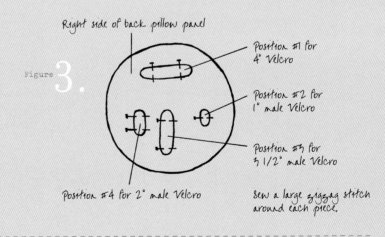

Figure 3.

Right side of back pillow panel

Position #1 for 4" Velcro

Position #2 for 1" male Velcro

Position #3 for 3 1/2" male Velcro

Position #4 for 2" male Velcro

Sew a large zigzag stitch around each piece.

Stuff the snail.

a. Turn the snail body Right side out, and press.

b. Fill the body firmly with fiberfill. Push the stuffing into the eyes and tail.

c. Fold the raw edges ½" under on each side of the opening. Pin, then slipstitch* the opening closed. Set aside.

Make the ruffle, and attach it to the shell's front.
(FIGURE 2)

a. First, place two ruffle strips Right sides together, matching one of the short ends, and pin in place. Stitch a ½" seam across the matched edges, backstitching at each end. Press the seam allowance open. Repeat to attach the other two ruffle strips together.

b. Fold the first ruffle in half lengthwise with Right sides together, matching the long edges, and pin in place. Stitch a ½" seam down the long edge and across both short ends, leaving a 4" opening centered on the long edge, and back-stitching at each end.

c. Trim the corners in the seam allowance, making sure not to clip the stitching. Turn the ruffle Right side out, using a turning tool* to push out the corners. Press the ruffle flat.

d. Fold one short end to the long folded edge, forming a tri-angle. Pin it in place. Sew a ½" gathering stitch* the length of the long folded edge. Pull the bobbin thread to gather the ruffle until it measures 28" long. Secure the gathering threads by placing a straight pin next to the end of the stitching. Make a figure eight a few times around the pin with the ends of the thread.

e. Repeat to make the second ruffle, starting by folding over the opposite short end to form a triangle.

f. Attach the first ruffle to the Right side of the first front pil-low panel. Starting in the middle of the swirl, place the pointed end of the ruffle with folded end facing the pillow panel. Match the gathering stitch to the marked swirl, and pin the ruffle in place. Sew on top of the gathering stitches, backstitching at each end. (FIGURE 2)

g. Repeat to attach the second ruffle to the other front pillow panel.

Attach the Velcro to the back pillow panels. (FIGURE 3)

a. Use the pattern piece as a guide. Starting on the first back pillow panel, pin in place:

- 4" piece of male Velcro in position #1
- 1" piece of male Velcro in position #2
- 3 ½" piece of male Velcro in position #3
- 2" piece of male Velcro in position #4

Sew a large zigzag stitch completely around each piece.

b. On the second back pillow panel, attach a 4" piece of female Velcro in position #1. Attach the other male Velcro pieces on the second back pillow panel as above.

Sew the shell pillows.

a. Place one front and one back pillow panel Right sides together. Pin around the edges.

b. Stitch a ½" seam around the pillow, leaving a 4" opening, and backstitching at each end. Trim the seam allowance to ¼".

c. Repeat to make the second shell pillow.

Stuff the pillows.

a. Turn the pillow Right side out and press flat. Loosely stuff the pillow with fiberfill. Do not overstuff. Fold the opening's seam allowance under by ½". Pin and slipstitch the opening closed.

b. Repeat to stuff the second shell pillow.

Tack down the ruffle.

a. Attach the backside of ruffle to the front pillow panel. Tack the ruffle every 2" to 3" around the outside edge near the edge of the pillow, using small hand-stitching. Repeat to tack the ruffle to the second pillow.

b. Match the Velcro on the pillows to the front and back of the snail, and at the top of the pillows.

O.

QUICK-CHANGE TABLETOP SET

changing cushion finished size: 20" wide x 32" long x 3" tall
soft removable pad finished size:: 12 ½" wide x 27 ½" long
difficulty level: 5

Here's the ideal changing pad for baby. It's soft, durable, and can be used on any stable surface—and it's as pretty or plain as you please. A great tool pocket hangs from the open end, offering easy access to diapers and wipes. Lightweight and easy-to-clean bumpers attach and pull off with Velcro.

FABRICS

* 3 ½ yards (44" or 54" wide) mid-weight print for the cushion, pocket, binding, and bolster covers
* ⅞ yard (44" wide) flannel for the pad

OTHER SUPPLIES

* 1 ⅛ yards (20" wide) mid-weight woven fusible interfacing (we use SF101 by Pellon)
* ⅞ yard (44" wide) fusible fleece (we use Fusible Thermolam Plus by Pellon)

* 1 ⅞ yards (3" deep x 24" wide) high-density foam (available at most fabric stores)
* 1 package polyester batting, full- or queen-size, to cover the foam
* 5 ¼ yards (¾" wide) sew-on Velcro
* Electric carving knife or a serrated bread knife
* 1 large spool coordinating all-purpose thread (we use Coats Dual Duty Plus)
* Hand-sewing needle

* Masking tape
* Tailor's ham* or a rolled towel

NOTE

* Use an electric carving knife or serrated bread knife to cut the foam. Mark dimensions with a marker. Use long smooth strokes. *Do not saw.*

• STEP 1 •

Cut out all of the pieces from the fabric and foam.

a. Using a ruler and fabric marker, measure and mark the dimensions directly onto the Right side of the fabric. Cut along the marked lines.

b. From the mid-weight print, cut:
- 1 front panel, 23" wide x 35" long
- 2 back panels, each 13 ½" wide x 35" long
- 1 exterior pocket extension, 19" wide x 10" long

- 1 exterior pocket, 19" wide x 8" long
- 1 pocket extension lining, 19" wide x 10" long
- 1 pocket lining, 19" wide x 8" long
- 1 pocket band, 19" wide x 2" long
- 8 long bolster panels, each 4" wide x 33" long
- 4 short bolster panels, each 4" wide x 13" long
- 6 bolster ends, each 4" wide x 4" long
- 2" strips to total 95" in length, once attached at ends, for the pad's binding

c. From the flannel, cut:

- 2 panels (front and back), each 12 ½" wide x 27 ½" long

d. From the fusible interfacing, cut:

- 1 piece, 19" wide x 2" long
- 2 pieces, each 19" wide x 10" long
- 2 pieces, each 19" wide x 8" long

e. From the fusible fleece, cut:

- 1 piece, 12 ½" wide x 27 ½" long

f. From the foam, cut (see Note):

- 1 piece, 20" wide x 32" long x 3" deep
- 2 pieces, each 3" wide x 32" long x 3" deep
- 1 piece, 3" wide x 12" long x 3" deep

g. From the batting, cut:

- 1 piece, 46" wide x 38" long
- 2 pieces, each 12" wide x 38" long
- 1 piece, 12" wide x 18" long

h. From the Velcro, cut:

- 4 strips, each 31" long
- 2 strips, each 11" long
- 4 strips, each 2 ½" long
- 6 pieces, each ¾" long
- 1 strip, 28" long

• STEP 2 •

Prepare the foam

a. Place the 20" x 32" piece of foam on top of the 46" x 38" piece of batting. Center one long edge of the foam even with the batting's long edge. Wrap the batting completely around the foam. Trim the batting's ends so that each foam end is covered by only one layer of batting. Pin the batting's edges. Whip stitch* the edges together, enclosing the foam.

b. Repeat the process to cover both the long and short bolsters. Set them aside.

• STEP 3 •

Make the pocket. (FIGURE 1)

a. Place each pocket extension panel, pocket panel, pocket lining panel, and pocket band Right side up on the fusible side of each corresponding piece of fusible interfacing. Follow the manufacturer's instructions to fuse them together, using an iron's "wool" setting.

b. Fold under ½" on one long edge of the pocket band to the Wrong side, and press.

c. Pin the unfolded long edge of the pocket band to the top long edge of the pocket exterior, with the Wrong side of the pocket band facing the Right side of the pocket exterior. Pin the folded edge of the pocket band to the Right side of the pocket exterior. Edge stitch* along the folded edge of the pocket band, backstitching* at each end. Machine baste* along the pinned raw edges.

d. Pin the pocket exterior with the band and the pocket lining Right sides together, matching the top edges. Stitch a ½" seam along the pinned edge, backstitching at each end. Turn the piece Right side out, and press. Topstitch* close to the top finished edge, backstitching at each end. Match the remaining three edges. Pin and machine baste them together.

e. Place the pocket and the pocket extension lining together, the pocket's lining side facing the Right side of the pocket extension lining. Match the bottom and side raw edges. Pin and machine baste along the bottom and side edges.

f. Pin the exterior pocket extension to the pocket extension lining, Right sides together. Stitch a ½" seam along the side and bottom edges, backstitching at each end. Clip* the corners in the seam allowance*, being careful not to clip the stitching. Turn the pocket extension Right side out. Push out the corners using a turning tool*. Press. Pin and machine baste the top edges together.

g. Fold the pocket and pocket extension in half, matching the side edges. Gently press a crease at the center fold. Unfold the piece. Pin the pocket to the extension along the center crease. Stitch along the fold, beginning at the bottom edge of the pocket to the top edge of the band, backstitching at each end. Set aside.

Figure 1

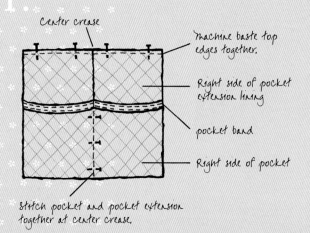

Center crease

machine baste top edges together.

Right side of pocket extension lining

pocket band

Right side of pocket

Stitch pocket and pocket extension together at center crease.

Figure 2

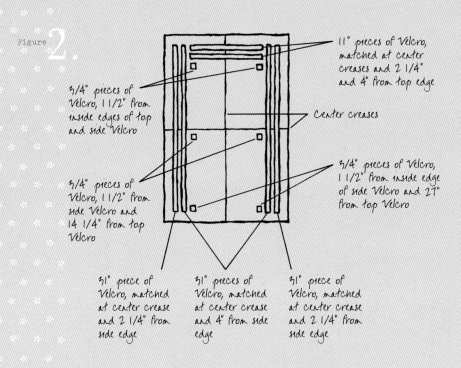

11" pieces of Velcro, matched at center creases and 2 1/4" and 4" from top edge

3/4" pieces of Velcro, 1 1/2" from inside edges of top and side Velcro

Center creases

3/4" pieces of Velcro, 1 1/2" from side Velcro and 14 1/4" from top Velcro

3/4" pieces of Velcro, 1 1/2" from inside edge of side Velcro and 27" from top Velcro

31" piece of Velcro, matched at center crease and 2 1/4" from side edge

31" pieces of Velcro, matched at center crease and 4" from side edge

31" piece of Velcro, matched at center crease and 2 1/4" from side edge

Attach the female Velcro to the front panel. (FIGURE 2)

🦋 **note:** All Velcro pieces attached to the front panel are female pieces. Male pieces will be attached to the bolsters and the removable pad.

a. Find the center of the front panel by folding it in half lengthwise. Gently press a crease on the fold. Open the panel. Fold it in half across the width. Gently press a crease on the fold.

b. Place the front panel on a flat surface, with the short end nearest you and the Right side facing up. Use a ruler and fabric marker to measure and mark the following guidelines for the Velcro placement. Measure and mark at several points for the placement of the long Velcro pieces. Connect the marks.

- Measure 2 ¼" in from the left long edge at several points. Make and connect the marks by drawing a line.
- Measure 4" in from the left long edge at several points. Make and connect the marks.
- Measure 2 ¼" in from the right long edge at several points. Make and connect the marks.
- Measure 4" in from the right long edge at several points. Make and connect the marks.
- Measure 2 ¼" in from the short top edge at several points. Make and connect the marks.
- Measure 4" in from the short top edge at several points. Make and connect the marks.

c. Find the centers of the 31" and 11" long Velcro strips by folding them in half, matching the short ends. Make marks at the center folds.

d. Place the first 31" length of Velcro along the outer left mark on the Right side of the front panel. Match the center mark on the Velcro to the center crease on the front panel. Place the outer edge of the Velcro even with the marked line. Pin it in place. Stitch completely around the outer edges of the Velcro, backstitching at each end.

e. Repeat the process to attach the second piece of 31" Velcro to the inner left mark on the front panel.

f. Repeat to attach the remaining 31" strips of Velcro to the outer and inner marks on the right edge of the front panel.

g. Place the first 11" length of Velcro along the top mark on the outer edge. Match the center mark on the Velcro to the center crease on the front panel, and pin in place. Stitch completely around the outer edges of Velcro, backstitching at each end.

h. Repeat to attach the second 11" length of Velcro to the top edge at the inner mark.

i. Mark the following measurements on the Right side of the front panel, using a fabric marker. (Measurements are for the ¾" pieces of Velcro used to hold the removable pad.)

- Measure 1 ½" down from the edge of the inner top Velcro and 1 ½" in from the edge of the inner right side Velcro, and make a mark.
- Measure 14 ¼" down from the edge of inner top Velcro and 1 ½" in from the edge of the inner right side Velcro. Make a mark.
- Measure 27" down from the edge of inner top Velcro and 1 ½" in from the edge of the inner right side Velcro. Make a mark.
- Repeat these measurements to make marks on left edge for the rest of the ¾" Velcro placement.

j. Place the ¾" squares of Velcro to the inside and under the marks on the right and left edges on the Right side of the front panel. Match the top outside corner of the Velcro to the measurement marking. Keep the Velcro straight, 1 ½" from the edge of the side Velcro, and pin them in place. Stitch completely around each Velcro square, backstitching at each end.

Make the back panel.

a. Turn under ½" on one long edge of the first back panel, toward the Wrong side. Press. Turn under again 1" toward the Wrong side. Press, and pin the inner folded edge. Edge stitch first along the pinned edge and then along the outer folded edge, backstitching at each end.

b. Repeat the above step to make the second back panel.

c. Find the center of the back panels by folding them in half, matching the short edges. Gently press creases on the folds.

d. Find the center of the 28"-long piece of male Velcro by folding it in half, matching the short ends. Make a mark at the center fold.

e. Place the 28"-long piece of male Velcro on the Right side of the first hemmed back panel, matching the center creases. Place the edge of the Velcro along the outer folded edge of the back panel, and pin it in place. Stitch completely around the outer edges of the Velcro, backstitching at each end.

f. Place the 28"-long piece of female Velcro on the Wrong side of the second hemmed back panel, matching the center creases. Place the edge of the Velcro along the outer folded edge of the back panel, and pin it in place. Stitch completely around the outer edges of the Velcro, backstitching at each end.

g. Overlap the hemmed edges of the back panels, matching the female to male Velcro. Match the folded edges at the ends. Pin them together. Stitch over both existing edge stitching lines at each end, from the end of the Velcro to the outer edge of the back panel, to close the seam.

• STEP 6 •
Complete the cushion cover. (FIGURE 3)

a. Place the completed pocket, pocket extension, and the front panel Right sides together. Center the pocket extension on the bottom edge of the front panel, matching the center creases. The pocket will lie against the front panel. Pin and machine baste along the matched edge.

b. Place the front panel and attached back panels Right sides together. Pin the outer edges. Stitch a ½" seam completely around the edges, backstitching at each end. Open the Velcro. Leave the cover Wrong side out. Press the seam allowances open using a tailor's ham or a rolled towel inserted inside the cushion cover.

c. Make gussets* in the corners. Place the Right sides of the front and back panels together, matching the side and bottom seams to form a triangle in the corner. Pin the seams together. Measure 1 ½" in from the point, along the seam, and make a mark. Draw a straight line across the corner at the 1 ½" mark. Stitch along the marked line, backstitching at each end.
(FIGURE 3)

d. Repeat to make gussets in the other three corners.

e. Turn the cushion cover Right side out through the Velcro opening on the back panel.

f. Insert the covered foam. Cover the male Velcro on the back panel with a strip of masking tape. (This will keep the batting from sticking to the Velcro.) Insert one short end of the covered foam inside the cushion cover. Push the corners of the foam into the cover's corners. Fold the foam in half and insert the other short end into the cover. Push the corners of the foam into the cover's corners. Push on the center of the foam to flatten it inside the cover. Reach inside and adjust the seam allowances to the center of the foam sides. Remove the masking tape. Close the Velcro at the center of the back panel.

• STEP 7 •
Attach the male Velcro to the bolsters. (FIGURE 4)

a. Find the center of two long bolster panels and one short bolster panel by folding each in half, matching the short ends. Gently press a crease on the folds.

b. Find the center of the four 31" lengths and both 11" lengths of male Velcro by folding each in half, matching the short ends. Make a mark at the center fold. Use a ruler and fabric marker to measure and mark the Velcro placement on the Right side of each bolster panel.

c. On one 33"-long bolster panel, measure ¾" in from each long edge. Mark at several points. Connect the marks, making a line. Mark lines on both long edges. Repeat for the second 33"-long bolster panel.

d. Match the center of the first 31" male Velcro to the center crease of the first long bolster panel, and place the outside edge of Velcro along the marked line on the Right side of the bolster panel. Pin it in place. Stitch completely around the edges of Velcro, backstitching at each end.

e. Repeat Step 7d to attach the second 31" male Velcro piece to the second mark on the first long bolster panel.

f. Repeat step 7d to attach the other two 31" male Velcro pieces to the second long bolster panel.

g. Repeat step 7d to mark and attach both 11" male Velcro pieces to the short bolster panel.

Figure 3.

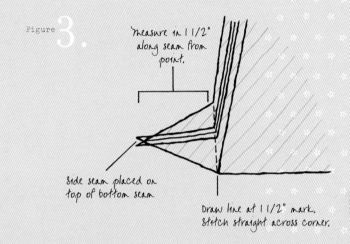

measure in 1 1/2"
along seam from
point.

Side seam placed on
top of bottom seam

Draw line at 1 1/2" mark.
Stitch straight across corner.

Figure 4.

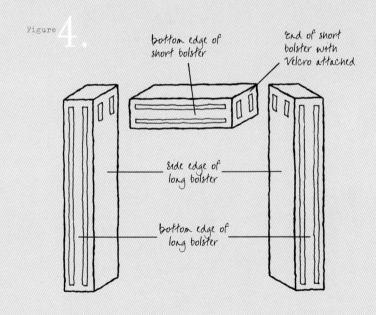

bottom edge of
short bolster

End of short
bolster with
Velcro attached

Side edge of
long bolster

bottom edge of
long bolster

h. On the third long bolster panel, measure ¾" in from one long edge and ¾" from one short edge and make a mark. Measure and mark ¾" from the same long edge, and 3 ¼" from the same short edge. Connect both marks, making a line. Measure and mark the line using the same measurements on the other long edge at the same end. Repeat to mark the fourth long bolster panel, making a mirror image of the third bolster.

i. Place the outer edge of the 2 ½" piece of male Velcro along the line, and pin it in place. Stitch completely around the edge of the Velcro, backstitching at each end. Repeat to attach another 2 ½" piece of male Velcro to the second line.

j. Repeat step 7i to attach both 2 ½" male Velcro pieces to the fourth long bolster panel.

k. On the first bolster end, measure ¾" in from one edge on the Right side and make a mark. Measure and mark at a second point ¾" from the same edge. Connect the marks, making a line. Repeat to mark the line on the opposite edge.

l. Place the outer edge of the 2 ½" piece of female Velcro along the first marked line, and pin it in place. Stitch completely around the edges of the Velcro, backstitching at each end. Repeat to attach another 2 ½" piece of female Velcro to the second marked line.

m. Repeat to attach both 2 ½" pieces of female Velcro to the second bolster end.

• STEP 8 •
Make the long bolsters.

a. Place the long bolster panels with the 31" lengths of Velcro attached Right side up on a flat surface. Using a fabric marker, lightly mark each edge in the seam allowance as right, left, top, or bottom (R,L,T,B).

b. Place the first long bolster panel with the 2 ½" strips of Velcro attached, and the right (R) edge of one long bolster panel with two 31" pieces of Velcro attached, Right sides together. Pin the long edges. Stitch a ½" seam along the pinned edge, starting and stopping ½" from each end. Backstitch at each end.

c. Place the first long bolster panel without Velcro, Right sides together, with the left (L) edge of the long bolster panel with two 31" pieces of Velcro attached. Pin them together. Stitch a ½" seam along the pinned edge, starting and stopping ½" from each end. Backstitch at each end.

d. Repeat to attach a second long bolster panel without Velcro to the opposite long edge of the first long bolster panel without Velcro, leaving 10" left unstitched at the center.

e. Repeat to attach the open long edges on the long bolster panels, creating a square "tube," stitching the entire seam. Do not leave an opening on this seam.

f. Pin the bolster end without Velcro to one edge at the end of the tube, Right sides together. Stitch a ½" seam, starting and stopping ½" from each end. Backstitch at each end. Turn and pin the second edge of the bolster end to the next short edge on the long bolster. Stitch a ½" seam, starting and stopping ½" from each end. Backstitch at each end. Repeat to attach both remaining sides of the bolster end to the short edges of the long bolster. Repeat to attach a second bolster end without Velcro attached to the other end of the long bolster.

g. To make the second long bolster, place the other long bolster panel with the 2 ½" strips of Velcro attached, and the left (L) edge of one long bolster panel with two 31" pieces of Velcro attached, Right sides together. Pin the long edges. Stitch a ½" seam along the pinned edge, starting and stopping ½" from each end. Backstitch at each end.

h. Place the first long bolster panel without Velcro, Right sides together, with the right (R) edge of the long bolster panel with two 31" pieces of Velcro attached. Pin them together. Stitch a ½" seam along the pinned edge, starting and stopping ½" from each end. Backstitch at each end.

i. Repeat steps 8d through 8f to complete the second long bolster.

j. Turn the bolsters Right side out, using a turning tool* to push out the corners.

k. Insert the covered foam through the opening in the seam, one end at a time. Push the foam into the corners. Adjust the seams by reaching through the opening. Turn under ½" on each side of the opening to the Wrong side, and pin the edges in place. Slipstitch* the opening closed.

Make the short bolster.

a. Place the short bolster panel without Velcro and short bolster panel with Velcro attached, Right sides together, matching the long raw edge. Pin the edges in place. Stitch a ½" seam along the pinned edge, starting and stopping ½" from each end. Backstitch at each end.

b. Pin the next short bolster panel to the opposite long edge of the short bolster panel with Velcro, Right sides together. Stitch a ½" seam along the pinned edge, starting and stopping ½" from each end. Backstitch at each end.

c. Pin the last short bolster panel to the attached short bolster panels, Right sides together. Stitch a ½" seam along the pinned edge, starting and stopping ½" from each end, leaving a 6" opening unstitched at the center. Backstitch at each end.

d. Place the two remaining long raw edges Right sides together, and pin them in place. Stitch a ½" seam along the pinned edge, starting and stopping ½" from each edge, backstitching at each end.

e. Sew the bolster ends with the Velcro attached to each end of the short bolster, following the instructions in Step 8f.

f. Repeat steps 8j and 8k to turn the bolster Right side out and insert the covered foam through the opening.

g. Turn under ½" on each side of the opening to the Wrong side, and pin the edges in place. Slipstitch the opening closed.

Make the removable pad.

a. Place the flannel back panel Right side up on fusible side of fleece. Follow the manufacturer's instructions to fuse them together, using an iron's "wool" setting.

b. On the Right side of the back panel, measure 1" in from each short end and side edge, and make marks. Measure 14" in from one short end and 1" from the side edge, and make a mark. Repeat this step to measure and mark on the opposite edge. At each corner mark, place a ¾" piece of male Velcro, matching the outer corner of the Velcro to the mark. Pin it in place. Stitch completely around the edges of the Velcro. Backstitch at each end.

c. At the center side marks, place a ¾" piece of Velcro, centering it over the marks with the outside edge 1" from outer edges of the back panel. Pin each piece, and stitch completely around both pieces of Velcro, backstitching at each end.

d. Pin the front and back panels Wrong sides together, matching the edges. Machine baste ¼" from all outer edges.

e. Refer to Glossary and Techniques (page 169) to make and attach the French straight binding* to the back of the soft removable pad, using a ½" seam, and finish the front edge of the binding.

Attach the bolsters and removable pad.

a. Match the Velcro strips on the long and short bolsters to the Velcro on the cushion top. Push in place to firmly attach.

b. Match the Velcro squares on the soft removable pad to the Velcro squares on the cushion top. Push in place to firmly attach.

chapter: 6.0 baby playtime

* IMAGINATION BOOK WITH STORAGE BAG * BUILDING BLOCKS WITH TAKE-ALONG BAG * CUDDLE KITTY TOY

Simple shapes and toys can stimulate and entertain babies of a very tender age. My favorite playthings for baby's earliest stages of wonderment include a cute and comforting kitty, soft, grabbable building blocks with a customizable carrying case, and an imagination book with striking black-and-white images. These pleasurable items for baby make for the best heirlooms.

DIFFICULTY LEVEL 2

IMAGINATION BOOK WITH STORAGE BAG ⇒

instructions: P.144

DIFFICULTY LEVEL 3

BUILDING BLOCKS WITH TAKE-ALONG BAG ⇒

instructions: *P.148*

DIFFICULTY LEVEL 2

CUDDLE KITTY TOY ⇒

instructions: P.153

imagination BOOK WITH STORAGE BAG

book finished size: 4" wide x 4" long x 1 ½" deep (closed); 4" wide x 4" long x 24" deep (open)

storage bag finished size: 5" wide x 5" long x 1 ½" deep

difficulty level: 2

Stimulating black-and-white designs of animals and flowers dance on the pages of this little, soft book that tucks away in a colorful fabric pouch. The washable gatefold book is a treat to fold and unfold, sparking visual exploration of happy, Chinese paper-cut designs.

FABRICS

* 6 squares, each 6" x 6", different mid-weight prints

* ⅜ yard (44" or 54" wide) mid-weight fabric for the bag's exterior

* ⅜ yard (44" or 54" wide) mid-weight fabric for the bag's lining

OTHER SUPPLIES

* ¾ yard (20" wide) mid-weight woven fusible interfacing (we use SF101 by Pellon)

* ¼ yard (44" wide) fusible fleece (we use Fusible Thermolam Plus by Pellon)

* 1 package printable fabric (we use Pellon Print n' Create Cotton Sheeting)

* Computer, scanner, and ink-jet printer

* 1 spool coordinating all-purpose thread (we use Coats Dual Duty Plus)

* Liquid fabric softener (we use Snuggle brand)

* Spray sizing or light, spray starch

* 4 ¼" (¾" wide) sew-on Velcro

NOTE

* The images (see Step 2) will have to dry overnight, so plan ahead.

• STEP 1 •

Cut out all of the fabric pieces.

a. First cut the Imagination Book pieces.

From 6 different prints, cut:

- 6 squares, each 5" wide x 5" long (for pages)

From the fusible interfacing, cut:

- 1 piece, 5" wide x 25" long

From the fusible fleece, cut:

- 1 piece, 5" wide x 25" long

b. Cut the Storage Bag pieces.

From the exterior fabric, cut:

- 1 panel, 7" wide x 12" long

- 1 tab, 3 ½" wide x 5 ¾" long

From the lining fabric, cut:

- 1 panel, 7" wide x 12" long

- 1 tab, 3 ½" wide x 5 ¾" long

From the fusible interfacing, cut:

- 1 piece, 7" wide x 12" long

- 1 tab, 3 ½" wide x 5 ¾" long

From the fusible fleece, cut:

- 1 piece, 7" wide x 12" long

- 1 tab, 3 ½" wide x 5 ¾" long

• STEP 2 •

Print the images.

a. Read the instructions in the Pellon Print n' Create package before beginning.

b. Using the images provided with this book, scan the images and print on the Pellon Print n' Create. Print the first image on one end of the first sheet. Allow the ink at least five minutes to dry, then turn the sheet around and print the second image on the opposite end of the same sheet.

c. Repeat to print seven images in total: 6 in black-and-white for the book, and 1 in color for the front of the bag.

d. Follow the manufacturer's instructions to rinse the images with the fabric softener—*do not skip this step!* Allow them to dry overnight.

e. Press the images, using spray sizing or light starch. (This will help further set the ink and avoid smearing.)

f. Center each black-and-white image in the middle of a 5" square, and cut it out.

g. Center the color image in a 4" wide x 3" tall rectangle, and cut it out.

• STEP 3 •

Stitch the pages.

a. Place the first and second images Right sides together. Pin one side edge. Stitch a ½" seam along the pinned edge, backstitching* each end. Press the seam allowance* open.

b. Place the third image and the second (attached) image Right sides together. Pin one edge. Stitch a ½" seam along the pinned edge, backstitching at each end. Press the seam allowance open.

c. Continue to stitch all six images side by side, pressing all seam allowances open.

d. Place the first print square and the second print square Right sides together. Pin one side edge. Stitch a ½" seam along the pinned edge, backstitching at each end. Press the seam allowance open.

e. Place the third print square and the second (attached) print square Right sides together. Pin one edge. Stitch a ½" seam along the pinned edge, backstitching at each end. Press the seam allowance open.

f. Continue to stitch all six prints side by side, pressing all seam allowances open.

• STEP 4 •

Attach the fusible interfacing and fusible fleece.

a. Place the print panel Right side up on the fusible side of the interfacing. Follow the manufacturer's instructions for fusing, using an iron's "wool" setting.

b. Place the print panel (with attached interfacing) Right side up on the fusible side of the fleece. Follow the manufacturer's instructions for fusing, using an iron's "wool" setting.

• STEP 5 •

Attach the image panel and the print panel.

a. Place the print panel (with attached interfacing and fleece) Right sides together with the image panel. Match the raw edges and seams, and pin together.

b. Stitch a ½" seam around all the edges, leaving 4" at the center of the bottom edge unstitched. Backstitch at each end.

c. Trim* the corners in the seam allowance, making sure not to clip the stitching.

d. Turn the row of pages Right side out. Push the corners out with a turning tool*. Press the edges.

e. Fold under the raw edges at the opening by ½". Pin them in place. Edge stitch* completely around the outer edges.

• STEP 6 •

Complete the book.   (FIGURE 1)

a. Match seams between images and prints. Pin in place.

b. Stitch-in-the-ditch* along the pinned seams. Backstitch at each end.

c. Accordion fold the pages. Press the book while it is folded, using spray sizing or starch. Place it under a heavy book overnight to retain folds.

Note: before printing on the Pellon Print n' Create paper, increase this image by 25 percent. (The 6 black and white images are in the pocket at the front of the book and are already at 100 percent.)

Figure

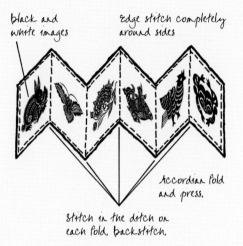

black and white images

Edge stitch completely around sides

Accordian fold and press.

Stitch in the ditch on each fold. backstitch.

Figure

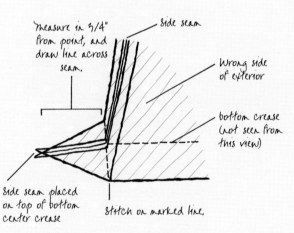

measure in 3/4" from point, and draw line across seam.

Side seam

Wrong side of exterior

bottom crease (not seen from this view)

Side seam placed on top of bottom center crease

Stitch on marked line.

Figure

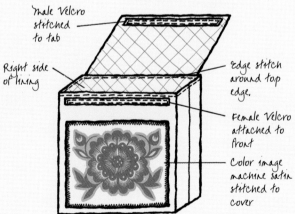

male Velcro stitched to tab

Right side of lining

Edge stitch around top edge.

Female Velcro attached to front

Color image machine satin stitched to cover

storage bag

• STEP 1 •

Attach the interfacings.

a. Place the exterior panel Right side up on the fusible side of the interfacing. Follow the manufacturer's instructions for fusing, using an iron's "wool" setting.

b. Place the exterior panel (with attached interfacing) Right side up on the fusible side of the fleece. Follow the manufacturer's instructions for fusing, using an iron's "wool" setting.

c. Repeat steps 1a and 1b to apply the fusible interfacing and fusible fleece to the tab.

• STEP 2 •

Attach the front image.

a. Place the color image 1 ¾" from one short edge and 1 ½" from each side edge of the exterior panel. Pin it securely.

b. Machine satin stitch, using a tight zigzag, around the edges of the image. Backstitch at each end.

c. Fold the exterior panel in half, Right sides together, matching the short ends. Pin the side edges. Stitch a ½" seam along the pinned edges. Backstitch at each end.

d. Press the seam allowances open. Gently press a crease at the bottom folded edge.

• STEP 3 •

Make the gussets* at the bottom corners. (FIGURE 2)

a. Fold one side seam down to meet the bottom crease, forming a point.

b. Measure and mark ¾" in from the seam's point. Draw a line across the seam at the mark. Pin and stitch along the line, backstitching at each end.

c. Repeat to make the gusset on the opposite corner at the seam.

d. Turn the exterior Right side out.

• STEP 4 •

Make the lining.

a. Fold the lining panel in half, Right sides together, matching the short ends. Pin the side edges. Stitch a ½" seam along the pinned edges, backstitching at each end.

b. Press the seam allowances open. Gently press a crease on the fold at the bottom edge.

c. Repeat step 3 to make gussets at both bottom corners of the lining. Do not turn Right side out.

• STEP 5 •

Make the tab.

a. Place the tab panels Right sides together, matching the raw edges, and pin them in place.

b. Stitch a ½" seam on three sides, leaving one long edge unstitched. Backstitch at each end.

c. Trim the corners in the seam allowance, making sure not to clip the stitching.

d. Turn the tab Right side out. Use a turning tool to push out the corners. Press.

e. Apply the 4 ¼" strip of male Velcro to the finished long edge of the tab lining, ⅛" from the finished edge. Center the Velcro evenly between the side edges. Pin and stitch it in place, backstitching at each end.

• STEP 6 •

Attach the tab and complete the storage bag.
(FIGURE 3)

a. Center the tab on the exterior back, with the Velcro edge facing out. Match the raw edges and pin them together. Machine baste* ¼" from the edges.

b. With the exterior Right side out and the lining Wrong side out, slide the lining over the exterior, pushing the tab between layers. Match the top edges and side seams, and pin them together. Stitch a ½" seam around the top edge, leaving 4" in the center of the front unstitched. Backstitch at each end.

c. Turn the bag Right side out. Push the lining down into the exterior and pull the tab out. Turn the raw edges under by ½" at the unstitched edges. Pin them in place.

d. Edge stitch* completely around the top edge, backstitching at each end.

e. Pin the 4 ¼" strip of female Velcro on the front, ⅛" from the top edge, and center it side to side. Stitch it in place, backstitching at each end.

BUILDING BLOCKS WITH TAKE-ALONG BAG

building blocks finished size: 3 ½" cubes
take-along bag finished size: 18" wide x 23" tall (excluding strap)
difficulty level: 3

Customize baby's blocks in patchworks of fabric for a colorful playtime. Use the fun alphabet included with this book to personalize the take-along shoulder bag with baby's initial. Fill the bag with as many soft foam blocks as you can!

FABRICS

For Building Blocks

NOTE: There is enough material to make 9 blocks.

* ⅜ yard (44" or 54" wide) mid-weight fabric for print A

* ⅜ yard (44" or 54" wide) mid-weight fabric for print B

* ⅜ yard (44" or 54" wide) mid-weight fabric for print C

* ⅜ yard (44" or 54" wide) mid-weight fabric for solid A

* ¼ yard (44" or 54" wide) second coordinating mid-weight fabric for solid B

For Take-Along Bag

* 1 yard (44" or 54" wide) mid-weight print for front, back, and strap

* 1 ⅜ yards (44" or 54" wide) mid-weight fabric of a coordinating print for the lining and drawstring

* ⅜ yard (44" or 54" wide) mid-weight fabric solid or print for the appliqué letter

OTHER SUPPLIES

For Building Blocks

* ¼ yard (24" wide) 4"-thick foam

* Serrated bread knife or electric carving knife to cut foam

* 1 large spool coordinating all-purpose thread (we use Coats Dual Duty Plus)

* Hand-sewing needle

For Take-Along Bag

* 1 ½ yards (20" wide) mid-weight woven fusible interfacing (we use SF101 by Pellon)

* ⅛ yard (44" wide) fusible fleece for the strap (we use Fusible Thermolam Plus by Pellon)

* ⅜ yard Wonder-Under or similar fusible webbing for the appliqué letter

* Letter of choice from alphabet included with this book. Copy and enlarge 725 percent.

* Large safety pin

building blocks

• STEP 1 •

Cut out all of the fabric pieces for the nine blocks.

a. From print A, cut:

- 18 squares, each 2 ¾" wide x 2 ¾" long
- 18 strips, each 2 ⅛" wide x 4 ½" long

b. From print B, cut:

- 18 squares, each 2 ¾" wide x 2 ¾" long
- 18 strips, each 2 ¼" wide x 4 ½" long

c. From print C, cut:

- 9 squares, each 4 ½" wide x 4 ½" long
- 18 strips, each 2 ⅛" wide x 4 ½" long

d. From solid A, cut:

- 9 squares, each 4 ½" wide x 4 ½" long
- 18 squares, each 2 ¾" wide x 2 ¾" long

e. From solid B, cut:

- 18 squares, each 2 ¾" wide x 2 ¾" long

f. From foam, cut:

- 9 cubes, each 4" wide x 4" long x 4" tall

🦋 **note:** The foam is cut larger than the finished block, as it will be compressed when inserted in its cover. Measure and mark the foam with a pen, and use a serrated bread knife or electric carving knife to cut it. Make long smooth slices—*do not saw it.*

• STEP 2 •

Make the pieced sides.

🦋 **note:** There are three different pieced sides in each block, a repeat of one of the pieced sides, and two un-pieced sides.

TO MAKE SIDE #1: (FIGURE 1)

a. Pin one edge of a 2 ¾" square of print A and a 2 ¾" square solid A, sides together. Stitch a ½" seam along the pinned edge, backstitching* at each end. Press the seam allowance* to one side.

b. Pin one edge of a 2 ¾" square of solid A and a 2 ¾" square of print B, Right sides together. Stitch a ½" seam along the pinned edge, backstitching at each end. Press the seam allowance to one side.

c. Pin a print A / solid A set and a solid A / print B set, Right sides together, matching the seam. Stitch a ½" seam along the long pinned edge, backstitching at each end. Press the seam allowance to the side.

TO MAKE SIDE #2: (FIGURE 1)

a. Pin one long edge of a 2 ⅛" x 4 ½" strip of print A and a 2 ¼" x 4 ½" strip of print B, Right sides together. Stitch a ½" seam along the long pinned edge, backstitching at each end. Press the seam allowance to one side.

b. Pin one long edge of a 2 ⅛" x 4 ½" strip of print C to the opposite edge of the 2 ¼" x 4 ½" strip of print B, Right sides together. Stitch a ½" seam along the long pinned edge, backstitching at each end. Press the seam allowance to one side.

c. Repeat to make another side #2, which will be used as a side #4.

TO MAKE SIDE #3: (FIGURE 1)

a. Pin one edge of a 2 ¾" square of print A and a 2 ¾" square of solid B, Right sides together. Stitch a ½" seam along the pinned edge, backstitching at each end. Press the seam allowance to one side.

b. Pin one edge of a 2 ¾" square of solid B and a 2 ¾" square of print B, Right sides together. Stitch a ½" seam along the pinned edge, backstitching at each end. Press the seam allowance to one side.

c. Pin a print A / solid B set and a solid B / print B set, Right sides together, matching the seam. Stitch a ½" seam across the long pinned edge, backstitching at each end. Press the seam allowance to one side.

Side #4 is the extra #2 already made above.

Side #5 is a 4 ½" x 4 ½" square of solid A.

Side #6 is a 4 ½" x 4 ½" square of print C.

Make the blocks. (FIGURE 2)

🦋 **note:** When stitching the 6 sides together, begin and end stitching ½" from each end. This will allow the top and bottom to pivot.*

a. Pin one edge of side #1 and side #2, Right sides together. Stitch a ½" seam along the pinned edge, backstitching at each end. Press the seam allowance to one side.

b. Pin one edge of side #3 to the opposite edge of attached side #2, Right sides together. Stitch a ½" seam along the pinned edge, backstitching at each end. Press the seam allowance to one side.

c. Pin one edge of side #4 to the opposite edge of attached side #3, Right sides together. Stitch a ½" seam along the pinned edge, backstitching at each end. Press the seam allowance to one side.

d. Pin the unattached edge of side #1 and side #4, Right sides together, to create a tube, connecting all four sides. Stitch a ½" seam along the pinned edge, backstitching at each end. Press the seam allowance to one side.

e. Pin one edge of side #5 to the top edge of side #1, Right sides together. Stitch a ½" seam along the pinned edge, backstitching at each end.

Figure

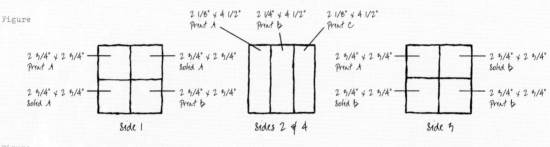

Side 1   Sides 2 & 4   Side 3

Figure

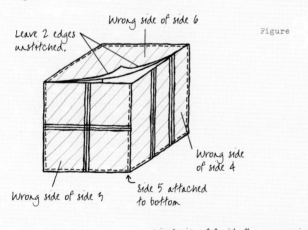

Leave 2 edges unstitched.
Wrong side of side 6
Wrong side of side 4
Wrong side of side 3
Side 5 attached to bottom

Figure

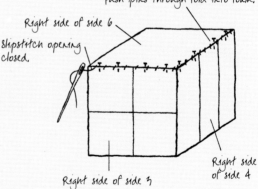

Fold under 1/2" on unstitched edges. Push pins through fold into foam.
Right side of side 6
Slipstitch opening closed.
Right side of side 3
Right side of side 4

Figure

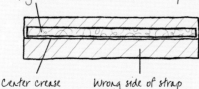

Right side of fusible fleece. Fuse in place.
Center crease
Wrong side of strap

f. Pivot, and pin the next edge of side #5 to the top edge of side #2, Right sides together. Stitch a ½" seam along the pinned edge, backstitching at each end.

g. Pivot, and pin the third edge of side #5 to the top edge of side #3, Right sides together. Stitch a ½" seam along the pinned edge, backstitching at each end.

h. Pivot, and pin the final edge of side #5 to the top edge of side #4, Right sides together. Stitch a ½" seam along the pinned edge, backstitching at each end.

i. Pin one edge of side #6 to the bottom edge of side #1, Right sides together. Stitch a ½" seam along the pinned edge, backstitching at each end.

j. Pivot, and pin the next edge of side #6 to the bottom edge of side #2, Right sides together. Stitch a ½" seam along the pinned edge, backstitching at each end. Leave the 2 final edges of side #6 unstitched until after the foam is inserted.

k. Trim each corner in the seam allowance, making sure not to clip the stitching.

l. Turn the blocks Right side out. Use a turning tool to push out the corners.

m. Repeat steps 2 and 3 to make a total of nine blocks.

• STEP 4 •

Insert the foam, and complete the blocks. (FIGURE 3)

a. Take one foam block and squeeze to compress it. Insert the foam into the block through the unstitched edges. Push the corners of the foam into the corners of the block.

b. Smooth the seams. Turn the seams along the top and bottom so they go down (or up) the sides of the block. (This will allow the top and bottom of the block to be flat.)

c. Fold the unstitched edges ½" under and pin them to the edge of the foam, pushing straight pins directly through the fold and into the foam. Slipstitch* the opening closed.

- -

take-along bag

• STEP 1 •

Cut out all of the pieces from the fabric.

a. Use a ruler and fabric marker to measure and mark the dimensions directly onto the Right side of the fabric. Cut along the marked lines.

b. From the first print, cut:
- 1 front panel, 19" wide x 24" long
- 1 back panel, 19" wide x 24" long
- 1 strap, 8" wide x 25" long

c. From the second print, cut:
- 2 lining panels, 19" wide x 24" long
- 2 drawstring strips, each 4" wide x 22" long

d. From the fusible interfacing, cut:
- 2 panels, each 19" wide x 24" long

e. From the fusible fleece, cut:
- 1 strip, 2" wide x 25" long

• STEP 2 •

Apply the interfacing, and prepare the letter appliqué.*

a. Place the front panel Right side up on the fusible side of the interfacing. Follow the manufacturer's instructions to fuse them together, using an iron's "wool" setting.

b. Repeat to apply the fusible interfacing to the back panel.

c. Follow the manufacturer's instructions to fuse the Wonder-Under to the Wrong side of the appliqué fabric.

d. Cut the letter from the enlarged copy. Place it Right side down on the Wonder-Under backing. Trace it onto the paper backing.

e. Cut the letter out from the fabric. Remove the Wonder-Under backing.

Appliqué the letter to the front panel.

a. Place the letter Right side up on the front panel, centered (side to side) and with the bottom edge of the letter 4 ½" from the bottom of the panel. Follow the manufacturer's instructions to fuse the letter in place.

b. Machine satin stitch around the letter, using a tight zig-zag stitch.

· STEP 4 ·

Make the strap and drawstring. (FIGURE 4)

STRAP:

a. Fold the strap in half lengthwise, Wrong sides together. Press a center crease. Open up the strap with the Wrong side facing up.

b. Place the fusible fleece strip on one side of the center crease. Follow the manufacturer's instructions to fuse the fleece to the strap.

c. Follow the instructions on page 172 to continue to make the strap. Do not turn under the short ends.

d. Place the strap on the right edge of the front panel, to the right of the letter. It should be 1 ½" from the bottom edge and 3" from the top. Keep the raw edges of the strap even with the side edges of the front. Be careful not to twist the strap. Pin, then machine baste* it in place.

DRAWSTRING:

a. Pin the short ends of the drawstring strips Right sides together. Stitch a ½" seam along the pinned edge, back-stitching at each end. Press the seam allowance open.

b. Fold each short end ½" in toward the Wrong side before folding it in half lengthwise. Then refer to the Glossary and Techniques (page 172), and follow the strap instructions to continue with the drawstring.

· STEP 5 ·

Complete the exterior.

a. Place the front (with strap attached) and the back Right sides together. Match the edges, tucking the strap between the layers. Pin the side and bottom edges.

b. Mark the drawstring casing's placement by measuring down from the top left corner (opposite from the side with the strap attached) and making marks at 1 ½" and 2 ½".

c. Stitch a ½" seam, beginning at the top left corner. Stitch to the 1 ½" mark, backstitching at each end. Begin stitching again at the 2 ½" mark. Continue down the side, across the bottom, and up the right side. Backstitch at each end.

d. Trim* the corners in the seam allowance.

e. Turn the exterior Right side out, and use a turning tool* to push out the corners. Press the seam allowances open.

· STEP 6 ·

Make the lining.

a. Place the lining panels Right sides together. Match the edges, and pin along the side and bottom. Stitch a ½" seam along the pinned edges, backstitching at each end.

b. Trim the corners in the seam allowances. Press the seam allowances open. Leave the lining Wrong side out.

· STEP 7 ·

Attach the lining to the exterior.

a. With the exterior Right side out and the lining Wrong side out, slide the lining over the exterior.

b. Match the top edges and side seams. Pin and stitch a ½" seam around the top edge, leaving 4" open at the center of the back. Backstitch at each end.

c. Turn the bag Right side out, and push the lining down inside the exterior. Press the top edge.

d. Fold the raw edges on the opening under ½". Press, then pin them in place. Edge stitch* completely around the top.

· STEP 8 ·

Make the casing, and insert the drawstring.

a. Topstitch* completely around the top edge twice, once 1" down from the top edge, and once 2" down from the top. Backstitch at each end.

b. Attach the safety pin to one end of the drawstring. Insert the pin in the casing's opening at the side seam. Feed the drawstring through the casing, around the bag, and back out the same opening. Remove the safety pin. Tie the ends of the drawstring together.

CUDDLE KITTY TOY

finished size: 8 ½" tall x 9 ½" long
difficulty level: 2

Modeled after my own very cuddly kitten, Birdie, this is a perfect naptime or take-along toy. Kitty's tail is just the right size for little hands to grab on to.

FABRICS

* 1 mid-weight printed scrap of fabric, 12" wide x 10" long, for the front of the kitty

* 1 coordinating mid-weight printed scrap, 15" wide x 10" long, for the back of the kitty and one of the stripes on the tail

* 1 third printed scrap, 4" wide x 6" long, for 2 of the stripes on the tail and the feet

* 1 solid scrap, 5" x 5", for the nose and ears

OTHER SUPPLIES

* ⅛ yard (17" wide) fusible webbing (such as Wonder-Under)

* 1 scrap lightweight fusible interfacing, 3" x 5"

* Tracing wheel and wax-free tracing paper

* 1 spool coordinating all-purpose thread (we use Coats Dual Duty Plus)

* Tapestry needle (size 20 or 22) for stitching the whiskers, eyes, and mouth

* 1 skein coordinating cotton perle embroidery floss

* 1 bag (12 oz.) Nature-fil (all-natural premium fiberfill by Fairfield)

* Sharp hand-sewing needle

* Seam ripper

• STEP 1 •

Cut out the kitty pattern pieces.

From the pattern sheet included with this book, cut out:

- Body
- Ears
- Nose piece
- Feet

• STEP 2 •

Cut out all of the pieces from the fabric.

a. From the first printed scrap, cut:

- 1 front kitty body

b. Flip the kitty body pattern piece over, and place the printed side of the pattern piece onto the Right side of the second printed scrap, then cut:

- 1 back kitty body

c. For the stripes, use a ruler and fabric marker to measure and mark the following dimensions directly onto the Right side of the fabric. Cut along the marked lines.

From the second printed scrap, cut:

- 2 stripes, each 1" wide x 3" long

From the third printed scrap, cut:

- 4 stripes, each 1" wide x 3" long

d. Follow the manufacturer's instructions to fuse the web side of the Wonder-Under onto the Wrong side of the third printed scrap, then cut:

- 1 set of feet

e. From the solid scrap, cut:

- 1 nose

f. Follow the manufacturer's instructions to fuse the web side of the Wonder-Under onto the Wrong side of solid scrap of fabric, then cut:

- 4 ears

g. From the fusible interfacing, cut:

- 1 nose

• STEP 3 •

Transfer the lines* and marks* from the pattern pieces to the fabric. (FIGURE 1)

a. Use tracing paper*, a tracing wheel* or chalk pencil, and the pattern piece as a guide. Transfer the lines for the placement of the nose onto the Right side of the front kitty body.

b. Transfer the lines along the edges for stripe placement on the Right side of the front and back of the kitty's tail. Draw lines between the marks.

c. Transfer the marks for embroidering the eyes onto the Right side of the front kitty body.

d. Transfer the feet placement guideline onto the Right side of the front kitty body.

e. Turn the front kitty body over, and transfer the stitching lines onto the Wrong side of the fabric.

f. Transfer the lines on the Right side of the nose piece for the mouth, nostrils, and whiskers.

• STEP 4 •

Make the stripes, and sew them to the tail. (FIGURE 1)

a. Fold the stripes ¼" in toward the Wrong side on each long edge, and press. Place the stripes between the lines on the front and back of the kitty's body. Pin them in place.

b. Edge stitch* down both sides of each stripe, backstitching* at each end.

• STEP 5 •

Make the kitty's face. (FIGURE 1)

a. Using a tapestry needle and cotton perle floss, embroider satin stitch* eyes on the Right side of the front kitty body.

b. Follow the manufacturer's instructions to fuse the interfacing to the Wrong side of the nose.

c. Embroider backstitch* the mouth, nostrils, and whiskers on the Right side of the nose piece.

d. Center the nose piece on the Right side of the kitty's body, easing it inside the guideline (the nose piece is larger than the guideline), and pin it in place. Machine satin stitch a tight zigzag stitch around the outside edge of the nose piece, backstitching at each end.

e. Stuff the nose. From the Wrong side of the front body, use a seam ripper to make a 2" slit through the front body, behind the nose piece. Fill the nose with fiberfill. Whip stitch* the opening closed.

f. Attach the ears. Remove the paper backing from the ears. Place the Wrong webbed side of the ears on the Right side of the front and back of the body, inside the guidelines. Follow the manufacturer's instructions to fuse the ears in place. Machine satin stitch a tight zigzag around the inside edge of each ear.

g. Attach the feet to the front of the body. Remove the paper backing from the feet. Place the Wrong (webbed) side of the feet on the Right side of the body, and fuse in place. Machine satin stitch across the top of the feet.

• STEP 6 •

Sew the kitty's body. (FIGURE 2)

a. Place the front and back of the kitty's body Right sides together. Match the ear pieces and stripes on the tail, and pin around the body. Sew along the transferred stitching lines on the Wrong side of body, leaving a 2 ½" opening under the tail, and backstitch at each end.

b. Trim the seam allowances to ¼", and trim each foot to separate the feet. Clip* into the seam allowance around the curves every ½" to ¾" and at corners, making sure not to clip the stitching.

Stuff the kitty.

a. Turn the kitty body Right side out. Use a turning tool* to push out the ears, tail, and feet. Press.

b. Firmly stuff the body with fiberfill, pushing it into the ears, feet, and tail. Fold the raw edges of the opening ½" under. Pin, then slipstitch* the opening closed.

Figure

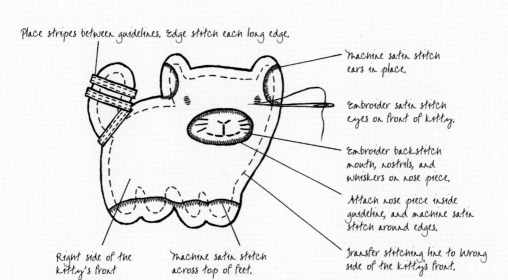

Place stripes between guidelines. Edge stitch each long edge.

machine satin stitch ears in place.

Embroider satin stitch eyes on front of kitty.

Embroider backstitch mouth, nostrils, and whiskers on nose piece.

Attach nose piece inside guideline, and machine satin stitch around edges.

Transfer stitching line to wrong side of the kitty's front.

Right side of the kitty's front

machine satin stitch across top of feet.

Figure

Place front and back kitty Right sides together.

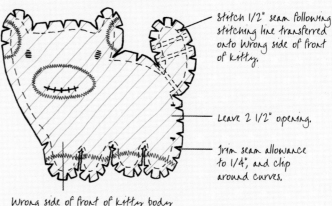

Stitch 1/2" seam following stitching line transferred onto wrong side of front of kitty.

Leave 2 1/2" opening.

Trim seam allowance to 1/4", and clip around curves.

Wrong side of front of kitty body

chapter: 7.0 baby memories

* BRAG BOOK * ALL IN THE FAMILY PHOTO ALBUM

here's a little something for Mom (and Dad and Grandma and Grandpa). Nothing is more personal than baby's first photos, and a personalized brag book is a must-have. Another lovely idea is to create a personal photo album for baby to keep and later show to loved ones. These great gifts are fun to make and will preserve family heritage for happy generations to come.

S.

DIFFICULTY LEVEL 1

BRAG BOOK ⇒

instructions: *P.162*

t.

DIFFICULTY LEVEL 4

ALL IN THE FAMILY PHOTO ALBUM ⟹

instructions: P.165

BraG BOOK

finished size: 5" square (closed); 5" wide x 30" long (open)
difficulty level: 1

You'll impress family and friends with baby's high cute factor (and your creative skills) when you whip out this gatefold, quickie brag book that lets you show multiple images at once. A snap to make, this tot tome is part simple paper craft and part simple sewing and can be easily customized.

FABRICS

* One 7" x 14" scrap printed fabric for the front and back cover
* One 6" square scrap coordinating solid for the heart appliqué

OTHER SUPPLIES

* One 6" square piece Wonder-Under or similar fusible webbing
* Pencil
* X-Acto knife
* Metal ruler
* 1 sheet, 22" x 30", 92-lb. hot-press Cover paper
* 1 sheet ¼" chipboard
* 1 spool coordinating all-purpose thread (we use Coats Dual Duty Plus)
* Scrapbooking glue (we use WackyTac Quick Dry Craft Bond by K&Company)
* Ten 3" square photographs (black and white or sepia)
* Double-sided Scotch brand tape
* Scrap piece of cardboard
* ⅝ yard (½" wide) coordinating ribbon

• STEP 1 •
Cut out the pattern piece.

From the pattern sheet included with this book, cut out:

- Heart appliqué

• STEP 2 •
Cut out all of the parts needed for the book.

a. Using a ruler and a fabric marker, measure and mark the following dimensions directly onto the Right side of the fabric. Cut along the marked lines.

From the printed fabric, cut:

- 1 front cover, 7" square
- 1 back cover, 7" square

b. With the coordinating solid fabric, follow the manufacturer's instructions to fuse the Wonder-Under to the Wrong side of the fabric, then cut:

- 1 heart appliqué, using the pattern piece. (Place the pattern Right side up on the Right side of the fabric.)

c. Use a pencil, X-Acto knife, and a metal ruler to cut the paper and chipboard.

From the cover paper, cut:

- 1 piece, 5" wide x 30" long

From the chipboard, cut:

- 2 pieces, each 5" square

Make the front cover. (FIGURE 1)

a. Remove the paper backing from the heart's webbed side. Place the Wrong side of the heart on the Right side of the front cover, matching the right edge and bottom corner of each. Follow the manufacturer's instructions to fuse the appliqué to the cover. Machine satin stitch a tight zigzag around both curved edges of the heart.

note: If the print from the front cover shows through the solid color heart, cut and fuse another heart to the back of the first one.

b. Spread the glue evenly on one side of one of the chipboard pieces, using a small piece of cardboard to smooth out the glue. Place the front cover Wrong side up on a flat surface, then center the glued side of the chipboard on top of the cover. Press them together firmly, turn them over, and smooth the fabric over the chipboard.

c. Spread glue on a 1" border on the other side of the chipboard. Fold the edge of the cover over to the other side, and press the fabric to the glued edge. Match the fabric at each corner of the front cover, making the extra fabric into triangles, and press firmly in place.

d. Cut off the surplus-fabric triangles, leaving ⅛" at each corner. Fold over the cut edges at each corner and glue them in place. Place a heavy book on the front cover until the glue dries.

Make the back cover.

a. Fold the back cover in half lengthwise, and then across the width, to find the center. Press a crease. Then open up the panel.

b. Measure and mark 9" in from one edge of the ribbon.

c. On the Right side of the back cover, match the 9" mark on the ribbon to the center of the back cover, laying the 9" of ribbon off the left side of the back panel. Pin the ribbon in place. Stitch a couple of times over the ribbon to secure it to the back.

d. Repeat steps 3b through 3d to glue the back cover to the second piece of chipboard.

Fold the paper to form the pages.

a. Using a ruler and pencil, measure and mark every 5" across the top and bottom long edges of the paper.

b. With a metal ruler, line up the first marks at the top and bottom of the paper. Hold the ruler firmly in place, and fold the paper toward you, along the edge of the ruler, to crease the paper.

c. Turn the paper over. Match the second set of marks. Hold the ruler firmly in place, and fold the paper toward you.

d. Repeat this process to fold the rest of the length of paper into accordion-pleated pages.

Attach the photos.

a. With the paper folded, lightly draw an X across the top and bottom pages (to remind you not to put photos on these pages). Unfold the paper and place it, "X" pages down, on a flat surface. Center a photo on each page of the folded paper. Use small pieces of double-sided tape to secure the photos in place.

b. Turn the paper over. On each of the remaining four pages, center another photo. Hold the paper up to light to line up each photo with the one on the other side. Put a small piece of tape in the center of each photo to secure it.

c. Machine stitch the photos to the pages with large zigzag stitches through both photos, backstitching* at each end. Each end page has only one photo.

• STEP 7 •

Attach the pages to the covers.

a. Spread glue on the "X" side of the first page, using a piece of cardboard to spread it smoothly.

b. Center the glued side of the page to the back of the front cover. Make sure the heart on the cover and the photos are facing in the same direction.

c. Repeat this step to attach the "X" side of the last page to the back of the back cover. Make sure the photos and cover are facing in the same direction.

d. Place the Brag Book under a heavy book, and allow it to dry completely overnight.

e. Uncover the Brag Book, and tie the ribbons closed on the right side.

Figure

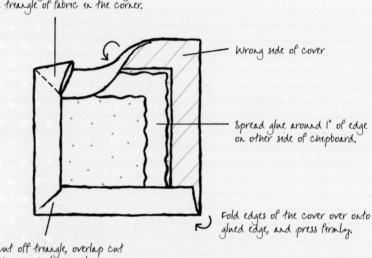

match edges on cover, forming a triangle of fabric in the corner.

Wrong side of cover

Spread glue around 1" of edge on other side of chipboard.

Fold edges of the cover over onto glued edge, and press firmly.

Cut off triangle, overlap cut edges, and glue in place.

t.

aLL IN THE FaMILY PHOTO aLBUM

finished size: 6" wide x 6" long x 1 ¼" deep (closed); 6" wide x 12 ½" long (open)
difficulty level: 4

This project combines family time and playtime, as baby gets to see photos of loved ones while touching and turning the soft fabric pages. This washable fabric booklet has easily customized adornments and Velcro closures.

FABRICS

* ¼ yard (44" or 54" wide) mid-weight fabric print for the cover

* ¼ yard (44" or 54" wide) coordinating print for the cover lining

* ½ yard (44" or 54" wide) third coordinating print for framing the photo pages

* 2 small fabric scraps with flower motifs for the cover 3-D decoration

OTHER SUPPLIES

* 1 ¼ yards (20" wide) mid-weight woven fusible interfacing (we use SF101 by Pellon)

* ¼ yard (44" wide) fusible fleece (we use Fusible Thermolam Plus by Pellon)

* 2 packages (four 8 ½" x 11" sheets) printable fabric (we use Pellon Print n' Create Cotton Poplin)

* Computer, scanner, and ink-jet printer

* 12 family photographs (ones with light backgrounds work best)

* Liquid fabric softener (we use Snuggle brand)

* Spray sizing or light, spray starch

* 1 spool coordinating all-purpose thread (we use Coats Dual Duty Plus)

* Handful of Nature-fil (all-natural premium fiberfill by Fairfield)

* Hand-sewing needle

* 4 ½" (¾" wide) sew-on Velcro

NOTE

* The images (see Step 2) will have to dry overnight, so plan ahead.

· STEP 1 ·

Cut out all of the pieces from the fabric.

a. From the exterior print, cut:

- 1 cover, 13 ½" wide x 7" long

- 1 tab panel, 5" wide x 3" long

b. From the lining print, cut:

- 1 cover, 13 ½" wide x 7" long

- 1 tab panel, 5" wide x 3" long

c. From the third coordinating print, cut:

- 36 edge strips, 1 ½" wide x 6 ½" long

- 6 center strips, 2" wide x 6 ½" long

d. From the fusible interfacing, cut:

- 1 panel, 13 ½" wide x 7" long

- 1 tab panel, 5" wide x 3" long

- 6 panels, each 12" wide x 6 ½" long

e. From the fusible fleece, cut:

- 1 panel, 13 ½" wide x 7" long
- 1 tab panel, 5" wide x 3" long

• STEP 2 •

Print the images.

a. Read the instructions in the Pellon Print n' Create package before beginning. Scan the My Family image included with this book into your computer. Print one copy on the Pellon Print n' Create.

b. Scan 12 of your favorite photos. Size them to 4 ½" x 4 ½" using photo-editing software (such as Adobe Photoshop). Print one copy of each on the Pellon Print n' Create. Print the first image on one end of first sheet. Allow the ink at least five minutes to dry, then turn the sheet around and print the second image on the opposite end of the same sheet.

c. Follow the manufacturer's instructions to rinse the images using the fabric softener—*do not skip this step!* Allow them to dry overnight.

d. Press the images, using spray sizing or light starch. (This will help to further set the ink and prevent smearing.)

e. Cut each photo so it is centered in a 5 ½" x 5 ½" square.

f. Center and cut the My Family image so it is 1" wide x 3 ½" long.

• STEP 3 •

Make the pages. (FIGURE 1)

note: Each photo panel is framed with print fabric. You will make six pages. These are stitched **Wrong** sides together, then turned **Right** side out to make three leaves. Each leaf will be folded in half, stitched in the center of the cover, and will have a front and back photo (for a total of 12). Determine the placement of your photos before beginning.

a. Place a 1 ½" strip on the top edge of the first photo, Right sides together. Pin. Stitch a ½" seam along the pinned edge, backstitching* at each end. Trim the overhanging edge of the strip even with the photo. Fold the strip away from the photo and press. Repeat to attach a 1 ½" strip to the bottom edge of the first photo.

b. Repeat to attach 1 ½" strips to the top and bottom edges of the second photo. Trim, fold away from the photo, and press.

c. Place a 1 ½" strip on the *left* edge of the first photo, Right sides together. Pin. Stitch a ½" seam along the pinned edge, backstitching at each end. Fold the strip away from the photo, and press.

d. Repeat to attach a 1 ½" strip to the *right* edge of second photo.

e. Place a 2" strip on the *right* edge of the first photo, Right sides together. Pin. Stitch a ½" seam along the pinned edge, backstitching at each end.

f. Place the opposite long edge of the 2" strip on the *left* edge of second photo, Right sides together. Pin. Stitch a ½" seam along the pinned edge. Backstitch at each end. Press the seam allowances* away from the photo.

g. Repeat steps 3a through 3f to make 5 additional pages.

• STEP 4 •

Apply fusible interfacing to the pages.

a. Place one photo page Right side up on the fusible side of the interfacing. Follow the manufacturer's instructions to fuse them together, using an iron's "wool" setting.

b. Repeat to fuse interfacing to all remaining pages.

• STEP 5 •

Make the leaves.

a. Place the first and second pages Right sides together. Match and pin the outer edges. Stitch a ½" seam around the outside edges, leaving 4" open at the bottom edge, to the right of the center strip. Backstitch at each end.

b. Trim* the corners in the seam allowance. Turn the leaf Right side out. Use a turning tool* to push out the corners. Press.

c. Fold the seam allowances under ½" at the opening. Press, and pin together. Edge stitch* completely around the outer edge.

d. Repeat with the remaining pages to make a total of 3 leaves. Set them aside.

Make flowers for the cover. (FIGURE 2)

a. Use a scrap of fabric with a flower motif. Cut around the flower, adding approximately 1" around the outside edge. Cut a piece of the same size from the scrap lining fabric and fusible fleece.

b. Follow the manufacturer's instruction to fuse the fusible fleece to the Wrong side of the flower. Trim around the flower shape, leaving ½" on the outer edge as a seam allowance.

c. Pin the flower and lining pieces Right sides together. Stitch a ½" seam around the entire flower, following the flower's outline. Use a small stitch, backstitching at each end. Trim the seam allowance to ⅛".

d. Cut a 1" opening in the lining only. Turn the flower Right side out through this opening. Push the flower shape out, then stuff it lightly with fiberfill. Whip stitch* the opening closed.

e. Center a ¾" piece of male Velcro on the back of the flower. Stitch across the Velcro in an "X" through all the layers.

f. Repeat to make a second flower of the same or a different size.

note: The flowers pictured in this book are both approximately 1 ½" wide.

Make the tab.

a. Place the exterior tab Right side up on the fusible side of the interfacing. Follow the manufacturer's instructions to fuse them together, using an iron's "wool" setting.

b. Place the exterior tab (with interfacing) Right side up on the fusible side of the fleece. Follow the manufacturer's instructions to fuse them together, using an iron's "wool" setting.

c. Place the exterior and lining tabs Right sides together. Match and pin one long and two short edges. Stitch a ½" seam on the pinned edges, backstitching at each end.

d. Trim the corners in the seam allowance, making sure not to clip the stitching. Turn the tab Right side out, pushing out the corners. Press.

e. Center a 3" strip of male Velcro on the tab lining, ¼" from the finished edge. Edge stitch around the Velcro, backstitching at each end. Set the tab aside.

Make the cover. (FIGURE 3)

a. Place the exterior panel Right side up on the fusible side of the interfacing. Follow the manufacturer's instructions to fuse them together, using an iron's "wool" setting.

b. Place the exterior panel (with interfacing) Right side up on the fusible side of the fleece. Follow the manufacturer's instructions to fuse them together, using an iron's "wool" setting.

c. Place the My Family panel on the exterior. It should be 1" from the right raw edge and 2" from the bottom raw edge. Pin it in place. Machine satin stitch completely around the panel, using a tight stitch, and backstitching at each end.

d. Place two ¾" strips of female Velcro on the exterior, to attach the flowers. For the top flower, the Velcro should be 1 ¾" from the top edge and 3" from the right edge. For the bottom flower, the Velcro should be 2 ¾" from the top edge and 4 ½" from the right edge. Pin the Velcro in place, then edge stitch and backstitch at each end.

e. Center the tab on the Right sides of the exterior front cover at the right, short end. Place the Velcro side facing out. (The tab will be attached to the front of the book when it is assembled.) Pin the tab in place, then machine baste it to the cover.

f. Place the exterior and lining Right sides together. Match all the edges, and pin in place. Stitch a ½" seam around the edges, leaving a 4" opening at the center of the bottom edge, backstitching at each end.

g. Trim the corners in the seam allowance. Turn the cover Right side out, pushing out the corners. Turn the seam allowances under ½" at the open edges, and press. Then pin the opening closed. Edge stitch completely around the edges.

h. Place a 3" strip of female Velcro on the exterior back, on the opposite end from the tab. It should be ¼" from the short, finished edge and 1 ½" from the top and bottom finished edges. Pin it in place, then stitch around the edges of the Velcro, backstitching at each end.

Attach the leaves to the cover. (FIGURE 4)

a. Open the cover. Center the 3 leaves on the cover lining. Pin them at the center strip, pinning through all the layers.

b. Stitch down the center of the wide strip. Sew through all the layers, beginning ½" from the top edges and ending ½" from the bottom edges. Backstitch at each end.

c. Fold the book closed. Press well, especially at the spine, to flatten the leaves.

Figure 1.

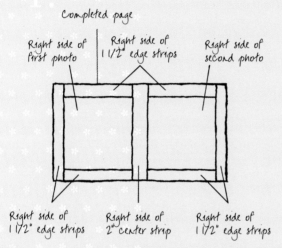

Completed page

Right side of first photo

Right side of 1 1/2" edge strips

Right side of second photo

Right side of 1 1/2" edge strips

Right side of 2" center strip

Right side of 1 1/2" edge strips

Figure 2.

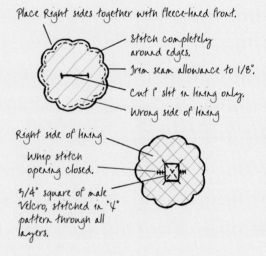

Place Right sides together with fleece-lined front.

Stitch completely around edges.

Trim seam allowance to 1/8".

Cut 1" slit in lining only.

Wrong side of lining

Right side of lining

Whip stitch opening closed.

3/4" square of male Velcro, stitched in "Y" pattern through all layers.

Figure 3.

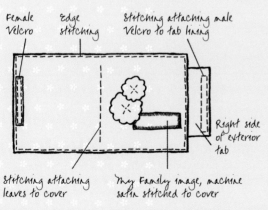

Female Velcro

Edge stitching

Stitching attaching male Velcro to tab lining

Right side of exterior tab

Stitching attaching leaves to cover

My Family image, machine satin stitched to cover

Figure 4.

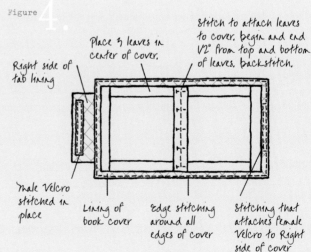

Place 3 leaves in center of cover.

Stitch to attach leaves to cover. Begin and end 1/2" from top and bottom of leaves, backstitch.

Right side of tab lining

Male Velcro stitched in place

Lining of book cover

Edge stitching around all edges of cover

Stitching that attaches female Velcro to Right side of cover

glossary and techniques

APPLIQUÉ: This is a technique in which pieces of fabric are sewn or fused onto a foundation piece of fabric to create designs. A tight zigzag stitch is used to finish the raw edges.

BACKSTITCH: This is used to reinforce stitching to keep it from unraveling. To do this, put your machine in the reverse position and sew three or four stitches.

BIAS: See *fabric grain.*

BINDING: A binding is the folded fabric strip used to finish the raw edge of certain projects, such as a quilt. There are three different types of binding used in this book. The following are instructions for each of these three binding techniques.

1. French bias binding, also known as double binding or French bias tape

Cut the binding strips on the bias of the fabric by first placing the fabric to be used on a flat surface, Right side up. Fold one corner Right sides together, matching one selvage edge with one of the cut edges to make a triangle shape. Press a crease on the fold. Then open the fabric and cut along the creased edge.

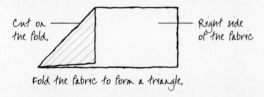

Starting at one end of the cut line, measure over the distance instructed in the project on the fabric's Right side, and make a mark. Make another mark the same distance on the fabric from the opposite end of the cut line. Match the 2 marks and draw a line using a ruler and fabric marker. This will create a bias strip the width needed for your project, parallel to the newly cut bias edge. Continue to measure and mark bias strips until you have the length called for in the individual instruction.

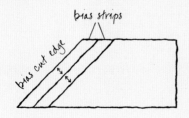

To join the strips into one long piece, lay the strips perpendicular to each other with Right sides together. Stitch across the diagonal edges of the strips with a ½" seam. Then, trim the seam allowance to ¼", and press the seam allowance open. Trim any small "tails" of fabric at the seam of the bias binding. Repeat until you have joined all of the strips into one long bias strip.

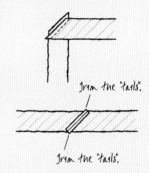

Fold the bias strip in half lengthwise with Wrong sides together, and press. Beginning at the center on one side of the project (do not begin near a corner), place the two raw edges of bias strip Right sides together with raw edge of the project. Leave at least 4" dangling free from the begin-ning point. Stitch the binding in place with a ½" seam.

Miter the corner: Stop stitching ½" from the corner, backstitch, and remove the project from the sewing machine. Rotate the project one quarter turn, and fold the binding straight up, away from the corner, forming a 45-degree angle. Bring the binding straight down, in-line with the next edge to be sewn, leaving the top fold even with the raw edge of the previous side. Begin stitching at the top edge and continue to the next corner. Complete all four corners in this way.

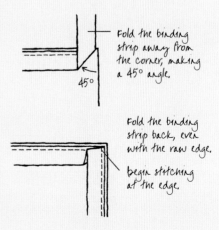

Finish the end of the binding: When you approach the beginning point, stop stitching, leaving the needle in the down position. Fold the beginning of the binding 1" back to the Wrong side and lay it flat against the edge of the project. Lay the end of the binding strip over the folded beginning edge, and stitch through all layers. Stitch 1" beyond folded edge. Backstitch at each end. Trim the excess binding. When the binding is turned to the back of the project, the beginning fold will cover and hide the ending raw edge.

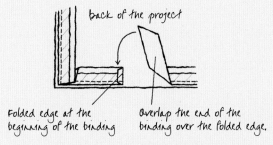

back of the project

Folded edge at the beginning of the binding

Overlap the end of the binding over the folded edge.

Bring the folded edge of the binding to the front of the project so that it covers the stitching line. Pin it in place. Machine stitch close to the folded edge to attach the front edge of the binding.

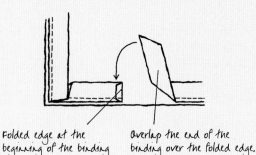

Folded edge at the beginning of the binding

Overlap the end of the binding over the folded edge.

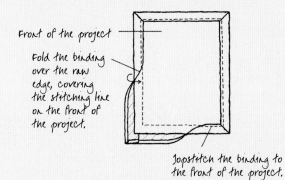

Front of the project

Fold the binding over the raw edge, covering the stitching line on the front of the project.

Topstitch the binding to the front of the project.

Turn the binding to the back of the project, and finish: Bring the folded edge of the binding to the back of the project so that it covers the stitching line. Pin it in place. Slipstitch the folded edge to the back of the project, folding the corners to create mitered corners.

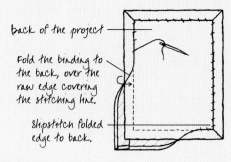

back of the project

Fold the binding to the back, over the raw edge covering the stitching line.

Slipstitch folded edge to back.

2. French straight binding

Cut strips for binding by cutting the width called for in the pattern instructions across the width of the fabric (not on the bias). Instructions to attach the binding, miter the corners, finish the end of the binding, and turn the binding to the back of the project and finish are the same as French bias binding.

3. Single-fold bias binding, or single-fold bias tape

Binding strips for single-fold bias binding are cut in the same way as for French bias binding. After cutting the strips and connecting them, fold one long raw-edge ½" toward the Wrong side, and press. Place the unfolded raw edge Right sides together on the back edge of the project. Leave at least 4" dangling free from the beginning point. Stitch the binding in place with a ½" seam. Miter the corners, and finish the end in the same way as for French bias binding.

BUTTONHOLE: To make a buttonhole, first measure the button you will be using. For example, if your button is ½" wide, you will make the size of the buttonhole (excluding the top and bottom finished ends) measure ½". Once you have figured out where you need to place your buttonhole, measure and mark the length of the button on your project with a chalk pencil. If you do not have a buttonhole setting or foot on your sewing machine, just use the following alternative method for making a buttonhole.

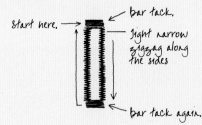

start here.

bar tack.

tight narrow zigzag along the sides

bar tack again.

Using the zigzag setting on your sewing machine, mark a bar tack (this means using the widest zigzag stitch and stitching a few times in place) at the top of the buttonhole measurement on your project with a tight and wide zigzag stitch. Sew back and forth a few times, then set your zigzag on a tight, narrow stitch to sew the first side of the buttonhole. At the bottom of the first side, reset the stitch for a tight, wide zigzag stitch, and sew a bar tack again at the bottom. Reset the stitch for a tight, narrow zigzag, and sew up the second side of the buttonhole. Set your stitch width to zero, and sew a couple stitches in place to "lock" the zigzag stitches and finish the buttonhole. Carefully cut the buttonhole open with a seam ripper.

CLIP: To clip allows some give in your seam allowance, especially if it is curved, in order to make the seam lie flat and make it easier to turn your project Right side out. When clipping, use scissors to cut into the seam allowance only, making cuts up to the stitch line, and taking care not to cut the stitching.

CROSSWISE GRAIN: See *fabric grain*.

DOT ON THE PATTERN PIECE: To use the dot marked on the pattern piece, first transfer the dot onto the Wrong side of the fabric piece by marking its position with your chalk pencil. Dots are used in a few ways. First, when you are stitching pieces together, you can use a dot as the starting or stopping point for the stitching. Second, a dot can serve as the point where you will pivot and turn the project before you continue stitching. Finally, a dot can identify where you should end a clip in order to easily turn the project Right side out.

DRAWSTRING: See *strap* for general directions. Specific instructions are included in each pattern for any changes or adjustments.

EDGE STITCH: An edge stitch is a very narrow stitch, done by machine close to the finished edge to finish a project, close an opening, or stitch something in place.

EMBROIDERY STITCHES:

1. Backstitch

First mark the shape as a guide for your stitches. Using a single layer of stitching, insert your needle up through point A and down through point B. Then bring your needle up at point C and down again through point A. Continue in this manner to the end of your marked line.

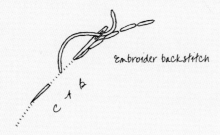

Embroider backstitch

2. Satin stitch

First mark the shape as a guide for your stitches. Insert your needle up at point A, bring it down through point B and out through point C. Repeat, making each stitch next to the previous one.

Embroider satin stitch

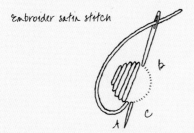

FABRIC GRAIN: Most fabric is made using a set of fixed lengthwise threads, woven at right angles with a set of crosswise threads. Grain indicates the direction of these threads. *Lengthwise grain* (also called *straight of grain*) refers to the lengthwise threads, or the fabric's length. *Crosswise grain* refers to the crosswise threads, or the fabric's width, and runs across the fabric from selvage to selvage. *Bias* refers to any diagonal line crossing either the lengthwise or crosswise grain. In this pattern, the *bias fold* refers to the diagonal fold of a rectangle of fabric to align one selvage edge (or an edge cut on the lengthwise grain) with one edge cut on the crosswise grain, producing a 45-degree angle fold.

GATHERING STITCH: Using the longest stitch on your machine and a loose bobbin tension enables you to pull the bobbin thread to gather the fabric.

GUSSET: This is a small square or triangular-shaped piece of fabric that is created by placing a side seam flat against a bottom seam or crease and stitching across them. A gusset will make a square bottom where there was only a flat-seamed bottom. Gussets are made in the Quick-Change Tabletop Set and the Imagination Book with Storage Bag (pages 128 and 144).

HAND-BASTE: Basting is used to temporarily hold two pieces of fabric together to prevent shifting while sewing final stitches. Basting can be done with pins, a sewing machine, or by hand. To hand-baste, place the two pieces of fabric in desired position. Then make a series of long, running stitches in the area described in the pattern instructions. Hand-basting is used in the Patchwork Crib/Playtime Quilt (page 116).

LENGTHWISE GRAIN: See *fabric grain*.

MACHINE BASTE: A machine basting stitch is used to hold sections of the project in place until you are ready to complete final stitches. Use the longest stitch on your machine, so you can easily remove these basting stitches later. You do not have to backstitch at the end of stitching.

MITER: The diagonal fold made at the corner in an edge finish, such as a binding, hem, etc.

NOTCHES: The notches are the triangle shapes along the cutting lines, which are used to match two different fabric pieces for correct placement.

PIVOT: Pivoting is used when you reach a corner or any place where you want to turn and continue stitching in a different direction. To pivot, stop stitching with your needle in the down position (keeping your fabric in place in the sewing machine), pick up the presser foot, and rotate or move your fabric to continue stitching in a different direction.

PRESSING CLOTH: A pressing cloth is a piece of neutral fabric. It is placed between the project and the iron to prevent shiny marks caused by the heat of the iron. You can also dampen the cloth when you want to create more steam to help press seams and press out creases in your fabric.

SEAM ALLOWANCE: The seam allowance is the fabric extending from the stitching line to the edge of the fabric. It can be pressed open or to one side as indicated in the project directions.

SELVAGE EDGE: The narrow, tightly woven finished edge along each side of the lengthwise grain of the fabric.

SLIPSTITCH: Frequently used to join two folded edges, slipstitching is nearly invisible as the thread is slipped under the fabric's fold. You will need a long piece of thread and a sharp needle.

a. To begin, feed one end of the thread through the eye of the needle, doubling the thread back on itself. Match up the ends, and make a double knot.

b. Insert the needle into the fabric, and pull the thread taut, hiding the knot.

c. Then insert the needle through a few threads on the other edge of the fabric. Pull the thread through until it is taut.

d. Now insert the needle back into the first side, through about ½" of the fabric, hiding the thread inside a fold. Push the needle through the fabric, and again pull the thread taut.

e. Repeat this process until you have stitched the fabric together, keeping even spaces between stitches.

f. To finish, tie off stitching by making a double knot close to the fabric and cutting excess threads to free the needle.

STAY STITCH: Stay stitching is sewn in the seam allowance before construction to stabilize curved or slanted edges so the fabric on these edges does not stretch.

STITCH-IN-THE-DITCH: This stitching, done either by machine or hand as indicated in the pattern instructions, is sewn in the groove formed by the seam. Make sure to line up any seams underneath so both seams will be sewn through neatly.

STRAP: *General instructions are the same for strap, tie, and drawstring.* Specific instructions are included in each pattern for any changes or adjustments. To make a Strap, follow the instructions below:

a. Fold the strap strip in half lengthwise, with Wrong sides together, and press a crease at the fold.

b. Open the strip, and fold each long raw edge in to meet the center crease, and press.

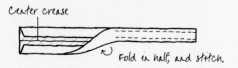

Fold the edges in to meet the center crease.

Fold in half, and stitch.

c. Then, fold the strip in half at the center cease, enclosing all of the raw edges, and press well. Pin the folded edges together, and edge stitch close to the folded edges on each long edge of the strap.

TAILOR'S HAM: A tailor's ham is a firmly stuffed ham-shaped tool, used to press seams around curved areas on a project. You could also use a folded towel to support the curve and press the seam flat. Tailor's hams can be purchased in most sewing stores.

TIE: See *strap* for general directions. Specific instructions are included in each pattern for any changes or adjustments.

TOPSTITCH: Topstitching is used for several purposes. It finishes the project and gives it a neat appearance; it is used to close openings left after turning a project Right side out; and it can be used as a reinforcement stitch, by adding another row of stitching to areas that will be used heavily and receive more wear. To topstitch, stitch parallel to an edge or another seam for the distance suggested in the project's directions.

TRACING PAPER: Paper with a coating on one or both sides. Used with a tracing wheel or chalk pencil to transfer markings from a paper pattern piece to fabric.

TRACING WHEEL: An instrument with serrated teeth on a wheel attached to a handle. Makes slotted perforations. Used with or without tracing paper to transfer markings from paper to fabric.

Transfer lines from pattern piece to fabric piece: On a hard, flat surface, using a tracing wheel and wax-free tracing paper, place the tracing paper with colored side toward the Right side of the fabric. Place the pattern piece over the tracing paper. Roll the tracing wheel firmly around or across the line to be transferred. Move the tracing paper to continue with a pattern or, if finished, remove it. The lines will show on the fabric.

Transfer marks from pattern piece to fabric piece: On a hard flat surface, using a chalk pencil and tracing paper, place tracing paper with colored side toward the Right side of the fabric. Trace over marks to be transferred, pressing firmly. Remove the tracing paper and pattern piece. The marks will show on the fabric.

TRIM IN SEAM ALLOWANCES: This technique reduces bulk around curved seams, so they will lie flat when you turn the project Right side out. Use scissors to cut off most of the excess fabric in the seam allowance. Be sure to press these areas once you have turned them Right side out.

TURNING TOOL: A turning tool is a pointed object, such as a closed pair of scissors, that can be used to push out the corners on a project after you have turned it Right side out. Specially made turning tools, usually constructed of plastic or wood, are available at sewing and fabric stores. When using a turning tool, push out the corners gently, especially if you are working with delicate, lightweight fabric.

WHIP STITCH: A hand-sewing stitch using overcast stitches. Stitches pass over the edge of the fabric diagonally. Whip stitching is usually used to close an opening that will not show in the finished project.

fabric reference guide

**ALL IN THE FAMILY
PHOTO ALBUM** (page 161)

Exterior:
AB14 morning glory
Color: mustard
From the Lotus collection

Borders/flowers:
AB17 wallflower
Color: apricot
From the Lotus collection

Lining:
AB17 wallflower
Color: mustard
From the Lotus collection

BED BUGS (page 22)

Butterfly:
AB07 coriander
Color: pink
From the Belle collection
(with coordinating solid)

Ladybug:
AB17 wallflower
Color: pink
From the Lotus collection
(with coordinating solid)

BRAG BOOK (page 160)

Exterior:
AB11 kashmir
Color: okra
From the Belle collection
(with coordinating solid fabric)

**BUILDING BLOCKS WITH
TAKE-ALONG BAG** (page 141)

Exterior bag:
HDABS3 wood fern
Color: olive
From the Nigella collection
(with coordinating solid)

Lining:
AB18 tree peony
Color: sky
From the Lotus collection

Blocks:
AB18 tree peony
Color: sky
From the Lotus collection

AB13 full moon polka dot
Color: slate
From the Lotus collection

AB20 temple garland
Color: sky
From the Lotus collection
(with coordinating solids)

**CHEEKY MONKEY LAUNDRY
BAG** (page 113)

Bag:
AB20 temple garland
Color: lime
From the Lotus collection
(with coordinating solid)

**COMFY JUMPER DRESS
WITH BLOOMERS** (page 52)

Bodice/bloomers:
AB22 oxford stripe
Color: apricot
From the Lotus collection

Skirt:
AB20 temple garland
Color: pink
From the Lotus collection

CUDDLE KITTY TOY
(page 142)

Front:
AB03 seeds
Color: royal
From the Belle collection

Back/stripe:
AB07 coriander
Color: ivory
From the Belle collection

Stripes/feet:
AB05 oxford stripe
Color: lime
From the Belle collection

CUTIE BOOTIES (page 56)

Exterior:
AB03 seeds
Color: olive
From the Belle collection

Lining:
AB07 coriander
Color: clay
From the Belle collection

EASY EMPIRE-WAIST TOP
(page 58)

Bodice:
AB21 lotus pond
Color: pink
From the Lotus collection

Skirt:
AB13 full moon polka dot
Color: cherry
From the Lotus collection

Bloomers:
AB21 lotus pond
Color: pink
From the Lotus collection

**THE EVERYTHING BAG—
TOOL KIT FOR MOM**
(page 86)

Exterior:
HDABS1 water lotus
Color: spinach
From the Nigella collection

Lining:
AB13 full moon polka dot
Color: lime
From the Lotus collection

**IMAGINATION BOOK WITH
STORAGE BAG** (page 140)

Bag exterior/1 panel:
AB05 oxford stripe
Color: lime
From the Belle collection

Bag lining/1 panel:
AB01 eyelashes
Color: lime
From the Belle collection

Remaining panels:
AB10 chrysanthemum
Color: blue
From the Belle collection

AB07 coriander
Color: ivory
From the Belle collection

AB10 chrysanthemum
Color: okra
From the Belle collection

AB07 coriander
Color: olive
From the Belle collection

KIMONO-STYLE PJs
(page 24)

Body:
AB07 coriander
Color: blue
From the Belle collection

Trim:
AB03 seeds
Color: duck egg
From the Belle collection

MODERN CRIB SET WITH STORAGE POCKETS
(page 20)

Sheet:
HDABS2 primrose
Color: lime
From the Nigella collection

Skirt:
HDABS8 starflower tiles
Color: ivory
From the Nigella collection

Deck:
muslin

Pillow front:
HDABS1 water lotus
Color: ivory
From the Nigella collection

Pillow back:
HDABS3 wood fern
Color: moss
From the Nigella collection

Quilt front:
HDABS2 primrose
Color: lime
From the Nigella collection

Quilt back:
HDABS1 water lotus
Color: ivory
From the Nigella collection

Quilt trim:
HDABS3 wood fern
Color: ivory
From the Nigella collection

Bumper pad exterior:
HDABS1 water lotus
Color: ivory
From the Nigella collection

Bumper pad lining:
HDABS3 wood fern
Color: moss
From the Nigella collection

MODERN DIAPER BAG WITH CHANGING PAD (page 88)

Exterior bag/exterior changing pad:
AB17 wallflower
Color: apricot
From the Lotus collection

Lining:
AB15 water lily
Color: clay
From the Lotus collection

Reverse side changing pad:
coordinating solid terry cloth

PATCHWORK CRIB/ PLAYTIME QUILT (page 112)

Front:
AB11 kashmir
Color: olive
From the Belle collection

AB05 oxford stripe
Color: blue
From the Belle collection

AB03 seeds
Color: duck egg
From the Belle collection

AB08 acanthus
Color: duck egg
From the Belle collection

Back/trim:
AB02 French wallpaper
Color: orange
From the Belle collection

QUICK-CHANGE TABLETOP SET (page 115)

Tabletop Set:
AB22 oxford stripe
Color: green
From the Lotus collection
(with coordinating solid flannel)

SLEEPY SNAIL WITH REMOVABLE SHELL PILLOW
(page 114)

Ruffle:
HDABS3 wood fern
Color: gold
From the Nigella collection

Pillow:
AB01 eyelashes
Color: lime
From the Belle collection

Body:
solid flannel

Stripes:
AB07 coriander
Color: sea green
From the Belle collection

AB04 henna paisley
Color: pink
From the Belle collection

AB01 eyelashes
Color: lime
From the Belle collection

SNUGGIE WRAP BLANKET
(page 18)

Front:
solid fleece

Back/borders/tie:
AB19 lacework
Color: grey
From the Lotus collection

TRAVEL BIBS WITH STORAGE CASE (page 84)

PIGGY BIB

Bib:
solid fabrics

MIXED-PRINT BIB

Front:
AB18 tree peony
Color: pink
From the Lotus collection

Back/pouch:
AB13 full moon polka dot
Color: camel
From the Lotus collection

Trim:
AB22 oxford stripe
Color: mustard
From the Lotus collection

BAG

Exterior:
AB22 oxford stripe
Color: mustard
From the Lotus collection

Lining/ties:
AB14 morning glory
Color: mustard
From the Lotus collection

TWO VERY CUTE HATS
(page 54)

BUTTERFLY

Exterior:
AB12 star paisley
Color: lime
From the Lotus collection

Lining:
AB15 water lily
Color: green
From the Lotus collection

Butterfly:
AB13 full moon polka dot
Color: camel
From the Lotus collection
(with coordinating solid)

MILITARY-STYLE

Exterior:
solid

Lining:
AB13 full moon polka dot
Color: lime
From the Lotus collection

resources

SOURCES FOR FABRICS AND NOTIONS

For a selection of the finest niche fabric retailers, please visit www.amybutlerdesign. com; search under Where to Buy for a retailer near you. Through these purveyors, you will find thousands of beautiful fabrics, as well as my fabric designs from Rowan, most of which I used for the projects in this book.

Visit www.westminsterfibers.com to see their full selection of amazing fabrics from all of their designers; you can also search on the site for retailers near you.

RETAIL STORES

Anthropologie
www.anthropologie.com
Wonderful selection of fashion and home goods. A great source of textiles with lovely prints for repurposing.

Blind Man's Bluff
1409 W. Third Ave.
Columbus, Ohio 43212
www.blindmans.com
614-488-8709
Bedrooms and lifestyles for the young and the young at heart! Great modern children's furniture and accessories.

eBay
www.ebay.com
Several online auctions and store sites for fabric.

Fairfield
www.poly-fil.com
Our source for premium products used in this book: Nature-fil fiberfill, Poly-fil Hi-Loft batting, Nu-Foam bumper pads, and travel-size Soft Touch pillow forms. Click on Where to Buy to find a retailer near you.

Fireflies and Fairytales
2132 Arlington
Upper Arlington, Ohio 43221
614-487-7885
firefliesandfairytales@yahoo.com
A children's boutique with unique clothing, toys, and accessories.

Fritzy Jacobs
635 High St.
Worthington, Ohio 43085
www.fritzyjacobs.com
614-885-8283
Designs and decor for the home. Great baby section!

Green Velvet
www.mygreenvelvet.com
Independent store in Granville, Ohio, that offers great ribbons, trims, new and vintage milliner flora, bead kits, and fabrics.

Hancock Fabrics
www.hancockfabrics.com
America's largest fabric store; varied selection of fabrics and notions.

Hobby Lobby
www.hobbylobby.com
Stores nationwide. Good source for foam, notions, and some fabrics.

Janome Sewing Machines
www.janome.com
Our sewing machine source. Click on Find a Dealer to locate retailers in your area.

Jo-Ann Stores, Inc.
www.joann.com
Good selection of flannels, fleece, and notions.

Nancy's Notions
www.nancysnotions.com
Great source for notions and specialty fabrics.

Pellon
www.pellonideas.com
The go-to source for several materials used in this book: Stacy's Stabilizer—SF101, Thermolam Plus—TP971F fusible fleece, Print n' Create Cotton Poplin printable fabric, single-sided fusible Peltex, and Wonder-Under fusible webbing.

Sobo Style
3282 N. Hight St.
Columbus, Ohio 43202
614-447-8880
www.sobostyle.com
A unique store specializing in old and new home furnishings and gift items, with an exceptional selection of children's goods.

Urban Outfitters
www.urbanoutfitters.com
Great source for modern prints, fun bedspreads, and curtains perfect for repurposing.

CRAFT SOURCES

A.C. Moore
www.acmoore.com
Large selection of craft supplies. Stores nationwide.

Dick Blick
www.dickblick.com
Huge selection of great arts and crafts supplies. Our source for 92-lb. hot press Cover paper and chipboard.

K&Company
www.kandcompany.com
Beautiful scrapbook papers and supplies. Our source for Wacky-Tac Quick Dry Craft Bond. Click on Store Locator to find a retailer near you.

Michaels
www.michaels.com
Great source for sewing and crafting supplies—huge selection. Stores nationwide.

GREAT CRAFT WEB SITES AND BLOGS FOR INFORMATION AND INSPIRATION

www.africankelli.com
www.annamariahorner.blogspot.com
www.craftster.org
www.craftzine.com
www.decor8.blogspot.com
www.dioramarama.com
www.getcrafty.com
www.heatherbailey.typepad.com
www.purlbee.com
www.quiltersbuzz.com
www.stacysews.com
www.worstedwitch.com

index